The Radio Set

by

Roslyn Schindler

the Peppertree Press
Sarasota, Florida

ISBN: 978-1-936343-91-1

Library of Congress Number: 2011929014

Printed in the U.S.A.

Printed June 2011

This book is dedicated to the men
in my life and their families.
Live, love, laugh, and dream.

Danny and Me at Pine Camp, 1951.

Prologue

The dreams of childhood don't always come true. I remember how much my brother yearned to see the world. We shared the same enthusiasm for foreign languages and travelling. I went to many countries when I grew up. Dan never did.

When he was little, his toy ham radio opened a new world beyond our door. He wanted to travel some day, but there were too many obstacles in his path.

People we love are here on Earth so briefly. I am painting portraits of each family member so they will live on in these pages.

Table of Contents

Chapter One
The Radio Set

I still cherish the picture I have in my mind of a boy sitting on top of his bunk bed with a microphone in his hand. My older brother, Danny, loved to play with the toy ham radio our parents gave him for his eighth birthday. When he spoke into the microphone, he was transported to exotic places around the globe. One night, he was speaking to someone in Cairo, Egypt, while on another, to a person in London, England. He said to his curious six-year-old sister, "I'm going to travel to all of these countries I'm learning about when I grow up."

"Me too," I told Danny. Whatever he did, I copied. He was my big brother and I always wanted to do everything he did.

Promptly at eight-thirty, Pop came into our shared bedroom.

"Can you tell us a story, Daddy?" I asked.

"What will it be tonight?"

"Mamie Pretzelheimer," we both chimed simultaneously. It was an invented tale just for us.

"Once upon a time there was a little girl whose daddy owned a pretzel factory. Mamie's braided hair resembled pretzels...."

Of course, the heroine of this bedtime story looked like me, a girl with small brown eyes and shiny chestnut hair. Her father's young assistant was the spitting image of my brother, a slim, blonde boy with brown eyes and a big dimple in his right cheek.

"All right. Lights out. You have school tomorrow," Pop said.

"It's so unfair that I have to go to sleep the same time as my younger sister," Danny griped. "My friends all have a nine o'clock bedtime."

"You share a room. Sorry," Pop chided. "Some day when you each have your own rooms, you can stay up later."

Pop closed the light and walked down the hall to the living room.

Our lives were so simple then. It was 1954. We lived in a small Tudor style home on a tree-lined street in Laurelton, Queens, New York. When we opened the front door, we went outside to play with friends on the block or around the corner. Our father went to work and left our mother to take care of us. All of the mothers in the neighborhood were home too. We went to elementary school, played after school, and did homework. On Saturday mornings, we watched our favorite programs: *My Friend Flicka, Lassie, Hop-Along-Cassidy, Superman,* or other kid shows like *Howdy Doody.* We felt safe and happy in our secure cocoon.

Neither Danny nor I realized a big change was coming. Pop was going to uproot us the following year and move us to California where his family lived. He and my mother whispered about their plans and stopped talking when we were around. We suspected something, but didn't know how tough the move was going to be.

One night before we went to bed, Danny talked about his third grade trip to Cushman's Bakery. I was very excited about going on a class excursion and wanted Mom to join the other class mothers to supervise us. I missed the trip to Cushman's Bakery. By that time, we were in California.

Chapter Two
Survivor's Guilt

I was still thinking about my childhood when my Aunt Sara interrupted my daydream and jolted me back to reality, the present time, nineteen eighty-three. The gathering in her Beverly Hills condo was anything but pleasant. We buried my brother in L.A.'s Pine Lawn Cemetery an hour ago in the pouring rain. My aunt invited the family and close friends to her apartment for refreshments after the funeral and burial. My husband, Scott, and I were going home tomorrow to New York. My parents were staying several days later to settle Dan's estate and empty out his small apartment of belongings. What did he have? Only a small bag containing a few pairs of cufflinks, his high school ring, a turquoise Navajo bracelet, a gift from his former girlfriend, Jan, a necklace with a silver coin, and his most prized possessions, the photographs he developed himself. When he was alive, you never saw him without a camera around his neck. I shuffled my position on the couch, trying to make my bulky body more comfortable. I

4

was in my seventh month, expecting a boy in May. Dan had promised to visit in June, but instead of him coming to us in New York, we had to fly to California for his funeral. My parents, usually so thrifty, splurged on a gleaming steel casket that held his body. My aunt was walking by sniffling as she wiped away tears and talked to guests, offering them more cake or coffee. "Eat, Darling, eat," she nudged me, but I couldn't put away any more of the ruggelach from the best bakery in Los Angeles as she described it to everyone. I barely acknowledged my parents sitting bleary-eyed opposite me on a love seat. My brother's best friend, Ben, approached to offer his condolences. I could tell it was awkward for him to make conversation with an obviously distressed woman he had never met before, but he wanted me to know that Dan hid his suicide plan from everyone. "Dan had his ups and downs. He was very direct with us at work. We all knew about the Bipolar Disorder and his reliance on meds. Sadly, he was having a very difficult time with depression and the side effects from the lithium he was taking. When he was working at the L.A. Dean Witter office, your Aunt Sara called a lot to check on him and sometimes came around to take him out to lunch or one of your uncles called and invited him to join them and their families for dinner. But, I think when his sales numbers were down and our manager moved him to the Nevada office, Dan had trouble coping with a new town, new people, and his illness. Sure, he drove back to L.A. on some weekend visits, but it wasn't the same. He missed his family and friends. He told jokes and put on a good game face for all of us, but he was hurting inside. He had me convinced that he was all right and said his shrink was giving him a new medication that was helping and I believed him. I wanted to believe it because I was busier at work, more successful, and had a new lady in my life. Dan didn't want to be a downer. I had no idea he would overdose on pills. He called me the day before and was his usual funny self." Ben shook his head as he related all of his narrative and I appreciated that he confided in me. His feelings assuaged the guilt I was feeling about neglecting my brother. What did I miss? Was I too occupied in my life to miss the signs of distress in my brother? Was he covering up his depression when we had upbeat phone calls about the new baby and his impending visit? Well, now, I was thinking as is customary in the Jewish tradition, our newborn son will be named for my brother. And, three months later, Alan Daniel Schindler entered the world bearing his grandfather's and uncle's names.

Chapter Three
Loss
(Back to New York)

Loss is tough to explain. My parents and I had our own coping mechanisms. They advised me to tell people Dan died of a heart attack. "It's simple. No one has to know the truth," my father recommended. "Besides, you're on a Sabbatical from school. Only your close friends will come to the Shiva at our house to pay their respects." My dad had always controlled all of us in our tight-knit family circle when we were under his roof. How was he incapable of controlling my brother? He talked to him almost every day, supported him long distance with small infusions of cash into his checking account. But, he didn't understand emotional carnage. He and my mother controlled their emotions. I saw their eyes were red, but they never shed a tear in front of me. Partly, it was a 1950s male mentality to resist crying and partly it was them. Their self-imposed stoicism was passed onto me.

Chapter Four
Honesty

Years have gone by. My boys are now men. And I have more time to contemplate a loss that resurfaces when a significant month approaches.

In March 2008, we celebrated my older son Jeff's engagement to Robyn. At the party, my husband's brother and extended family were seated at a table in the back of the restaurant. Scott made the rounds greeting guests. I sat next to my cousin, Rima, from California so I didn't have to answer questions from any of Robyn's family or friends about a brother or sister. I don't lie or flinch when I reply, "I don't have any siblings. My brother suffered from Bipolar Disorder and committed suicide." They usually stare uncomfortably when I give them the truth and mumble, "So sorry." It's painful for them and me, but it lasts for a minute. By sitting next to my cousin, I avoided the topic and was enjoying the party. She knew the whole story well. It was relaxing on the velvet dining chair. I breathed in the scent of fried potatoes, chicken Milanese, and pasta with a garlicky marinara sauce. I raised my champagne glass to toast the future bride and groom.

Chapter Five
Renewal

December brought more joy. We planned a New Year's Eve celebration for our Florida friends. We always made parties when we lived in New York and were continuing the tradition in our new home in southwest Florida. One couple was not going to share the occasion with us. They lost their only son on December 8, 2008 when his small plane crashed killing him instantly. He and my brother shared the same name and fate—death at an early age. My brother was 36 when he died and their son was only 40.

I was thinking about our friends' loss and taking down the 30-cup coffee pot from the cabinet above the refrigerator. I saw my brother's photo behind the magnet on the massive stainless steel icebox. I was organizing what I needed for the upcoming party and taking a few minutes to look at Dan's photo. He appeared frozen in time, a young, fit, handsome man in his 30s leaning over his balcony with a coffee mug in hand, clothes drying on the railing outside his second floor apartment. The mountains, a soothing mauve color, the baby-blue sky looking like a painted Hollywood backdrop. Clipped on top of the Nevada scene was a tiny school picture of him. It was taken before we finished our school year in Laurelton and still lived on 231st Street. I smiled as I recalled an incident from childhood. On this particular Saturday, Pop was working as a realtor and Mommy needed to do a little shopping for tonight's supper. She was taking us to Springfield Boulevard. "Hold your brother's hand, Rozzie," she told me. "I am going to be pushing the shopping cart and walking ahead of you to Bohack's Market." I grimaced about having to hold Danny's hand and my brother made a derogatory remark about girls, as a six-year-old would do especially regarding his pesky four and a half year old sister. But, we complied and like two chicks trailing after their mother, we tagged along in back of the shopping cart. Mommy was half a block ahead of us and reading the sale ads plastered on the plate glass window of the grocery store. She was checking her list and thinking about what she had to buy for tonight's dinner. It had to be served promptly at six after Pop listened to the evening news. My brother saw it first, a green paper bill lying on the pavement before our eyes. "Let's bring the dollar to Mommy and ask if we can buy some candy." I eagerly suggested the idea to my big brother who looked doubtful. "No, It's dirty and our parents always said not to pick up things from the street like those bottle caps I found last week and Pop made me throw them out." He convinced me not to touch the dollar and I was very disappointed. I respected his wishes. I didn't tell our mother either. Years later when I was a single girl in my 20s and visited my brother in L.A., I asked him if he remembered us leaving a dollar on the sidewalk because it was dirty and he laughed and said, "Yes. How innocent we were in those days." We both laughed until tears rolled down our cheeks.

Chapter Six
Coping with a Death in the Family

After my brother's funeral, Scott returned to teaching and I went back to the community college where I was taking classes for my Sabbatical Leave from my school. It was very hard to concentrate and I decided on Friday to cut my classes, go to my Brooklyn High School, and visit my best friend, Ellen. She and I were both Spanish teachers in a foreign language department dominated by macho Italian men. We were allies in that hostile environment and always watched out for each other Today, I desperately needed to speak to her. She sensed my dismay the minute I walked into her class.

"What's wrong, Mrs. Schindler?" she asked while her students stared at the intruder who barged in unannounced.

"My brother died. I went to his funeral in California and just got back two days ago."

Ellen was shocked and her students were curious to hear the details of my story. They were also glad to have a break away from reading aloud in Spanish. But, they needed to be kept occupied and, therefore, Ellen assigned them a few pages of grammar exercises. We continued talking.

"It's a pity that the Bipolar Disorder wrecked his life." Ellen knew all about my brother's struggles with his mental disease. I had described many of his suicide attempts beginning when he was still a high school student living at home. I had hoped he would get better while he was living in California, but was not surprised that a drug overdose caused his death. Once before, drugs were pumped out of his stomach and he was revived. But, a person doesn't have nine lives like a cat. I always knew he could not survive every suicide attempt. I was so devastated by the loss. Ellen understood. Her brother, Larry, suffered from Juvenile Diabetes and almost died several times throughout his life. She faced the uncertainty of her brother's survival too. My friend and colleague was the only human being with whom I could commiserate. Just being with her comforted me.

"How are your parents coping with the loss of their only son?"

"They're going to sit Shiva all week. If you can, come visit me at my parents' house on Sunday."

"Please give me directions to their house. My husband, Jack, and I will be there," Ellen said.

The class period was ending and the students were packing up their texts and notebooks. I hurriedly kissed her and exited the room before the onslaught of the masses in the hallway during passing time.

In the car on the way home I thought about Dan and his unfulfilled dreams. When we were children he told me he wanted to explore foreign lands. I remember him sitting on his bed and playing with that toy ham radio set our parents had given him for his birthday. Pop, a history teacher, explained that men used their ham radios to communicate with people from all over the world. He told my brother that our Uncle Lou in California conversed with a few men in England on his radio. Also he corresponded with them and collected foreign stamps. My brother was intrigued and wanted a ham radio just like Uncle Lou had. On rainy, leisurely Sunday afternoons, my brother held the earpiece of the radio set to his ear and spoke into the toy microphone. "Hello, Joe. How's the weather today in London? It's breezy and a bit foggy here in Laurelton, New York where I live." He made up the queries and replies of his fictitious overseas conversations and looked at his world map to learn about each country.

When my brother Dan and I were teenagers, we both studied foreign languages and yearned for an opportunity to go to the country where we could speak to the native population. We had Madame M. for French. She encouraged us to speak the language in class and with each other at home. I did travel to France when I was in college. Dan never went abroad. It was a shame. He loved speaking French. I sighed deeply and reached for a kleenex to dab at the tears coursing down my cheeks as I was driving the car home.

Dan's illness ruined his personal and work relationships. He was a stockbroker who sold very sporadically. When he was depressed, he sold very few stocks to clients. Fortunately, our aunts and uncles bought stocks he recommended. His personal life was in shambles. He was either charming or frightening depending on his mood swings. Dan's young wife couldn't deal with his wild behavior. She divorced him after a year. His girlfriend in California lived with him for more than two years and tried to make their relationship work, but wanted children and didn't want to risk having them with a volatile, unstable man. She left too. Dan tried to persevere alone, but was very unhappy. He ended his life after only thirty-six years on Earth.

I stopped thinking about Dan when I pulled into my driveway and turned off the ignition. My two babies were waiting at home with the housekeeper and I missed them. At the time, my busy life distracted me and I barely had time for mourning. I was working fulltime as a teacher and raising my two boys. After the Shiva period was over, I pushed thoughts of my poor brother aside and continued on with my life.

I have the time now to think about how much I have experienced so far. I miss my brother. My children are missing an uncle. When I go to my first-born son Jeff's wedding, I will think to myself, your uncle is not here to share this happiness with us. The family table will be a little emptier.

Chapter Seven
Drama, Remembrance of the Past

My brother taught me how to laugh. Our parents were relieved when they heard peals of laughter coming from my crib instead of the usual loud crying. My mother was exhausted from the nightly colic-induced screams I produced. No rocking or lullabies quieted me. But, one day my stomach matured and I felt better. My two year-old brother's crib was next to mine in our room. He was making silly faces to his best audience, me. I giggled and watched him, fascinated by his contorted features and absurd noises. My parents praised him for entertaining me and allowing them to sleep a little more in the morning. "She loves watching what you do," my mother said and picked him up to give him a bottle. Mine was warming on the stove. While he played with his toys in the crib, my mother fed me my bottle. And that's how it was, according to what my mother told me. She took care of two babies all day while her husband was teaching history at Far Rockaway High School.

"How did I give up my art career and become a diaper changer?" she asked her friend Ruth during a Tuesday evening Mah Jong game.

"We all stopped working and had children, Estelle. I was a secretary for a high-powered executive and made a good salary that I gave up when I married Eddie."

"I miss the work I did. I was earning more than a lot of men before the war. I was a top fashion illustrator for Macy's and my ads were in the newspapers every week. I loved going to the office every day. Now I knit sweaters for the kids. That's as creative as I get when I am not washing dishes or making dinner or taking care of babies."

There was little art, but plenty of drama in our lives. Our parents worked hard and planned getaways for the weekends and in the summers. We couldn't afford fancy hotels on a teacher's salary, but my dad figured out a way to go on trips if we camped out. On one summer camping trip to the Adirondack Mountains, my dad packed up the station wagon with all of our gear and stood alongside of the car with his checklist. He marked off each item as it went into the automobile. "First aid kit, Coleman stove ..." He turned to my mother and said,

"Let's go, Estelle. We have everything." We drove away from the house and reached the corner of the block when my mother realized it was too quiet in the back seat of the Rambler. She turned around and saw Danny in his seat, but they were missing one child—me!

"Oh no, you forgot to take Rozzie out of her crib and put her into the car, Saul." My dad was always nervous to do everything right and couldn't believe he made such a big mistake. He quickly turned the car around and went back to the house to get me. I was red with rage and tears streamed down my cheeks. I sobbed as I was drinking the bottle my mother handed me. My baby brother sang me a song and soon I calmed down and we both fell asleep as our father drove the car. My parents loved retelling this story. My mother laughed that I wasn't on a list, so Dad forgot about me.

Chapter Eight
Going West, 1955

Our school year was ending and we were happy to have a lazy summer at home. Our parents sat us down on the last day and informed us that we were going to leave Laurelton, New York and move to North Hollywood, California. My brother and I were shocked. We both started crying and ran to our room. My brother spoke first, "I don't want to leave our aunts, uncles, and friends in the neighborhood. I don't want to change schools. I like it here." I went to the kitchen to find our black cat with the luminous green eyes. I found him lying on the floor near the window and carried him to our room. We both sat on my bottom bunk bed and were petting the cat, Satan. Our parents knocked on the door and came in to talk to us.

"It's a big change, but you'll like California. We'll live in Grandpa's apartment building in North Hollywood. My brothers and sister all have children and you'll be able to play with many cousins." Pop was doing his best to convince us that it was going to be okay.

"It's a grand adventure. Danny and you will fly with our friends, Herb and Diane Greene and their daughter, Marla. They're relocating out west too. Your father and I are driving the station wagon across the country with some of our things that we need to bring with us," Mom told us.

I held the cat closer on my lap and stroked his fur and listened to him purr contentedly. "So you'll take our kitty in the car with you?"

"We think it's best for him to go to a new home. The car ride will be too hot for an animal and no hotel will allow us to sleep in their rooms if we have a cat with us," my father explained.

"Our next-door neighbors, the Browns, have one cat and will accept another in their household. Satan will live with their cat, Fluffy," Mom said.

"We'll take you to Disneyland when we get to Los Angeles. You will meet your favorite cartoon characters, Mickey and Minnie Mouse and you can go on all of the rides," our father promised.

Danny turned to me," Hmmm, maybe it won't be so bad."

"I guess," I said, very excited about the prospect of going to the Magic Kingdom in Disneyland.

The last summer we spent in New York was very nostalgic and one Danny and I never forgot. We played with the neighborhood children, drank lemonade, and bought ice cream from the Good Humor man who came to our block at least once a week. Danny and I played Red Light, Green Light with our pals. The boys separated from the girls to play Cowboys and Indians, shoot their cap pistols, and take turns dying. The girls played potsie and jacks on the sidewalk in front of the houses. The neighborhood mothers took turns watching the children play. While we ran around, they washed clothes and hung the wet laundry outside in the yards to dry. We loved running under the clotheslines even though our mothers scolded us. Sometimes a truck with a portable ride parked on our block and we asked our mothers for fifteen cents to take a ride. In the early evening when the fathers were home from work, the parents sat outside in their backyards and chatted while we kids ran after fireflies. We all brought jars with holes punched in the tin covers and when we caught some of the fireflies, we put them in the jars. We hoped they would continue to live the next day, but by the morning, their taillights were extinguished and they had perished. We deposited their remains in the garden and renewed our quest to capture them the next night.

August was approaching. Our parents had their plans in place for our big move. Danny and I were going to meet the Greene family at Idlewild Airport (renamed Kennedy) on August 15, 1955 and fly out to L.A. Our Uncle Sam and Aunt Shirley were going to pick us up at the airport in California. Danny and I were staying with our grandparents until our parents arrived by car a few days later. They were leaving August 2nd and driving across country in 14 days. When they had to go, our Aunt Bea and Uncle Morris took care of us in our home. The new couple that bought our house was not moving in until September.

The neighbors were sad that we were leaving. The friends next door made us dinner and invited other neighbors for a small going away party. We kissed everyone goodbye and promised to write.

The morning of the flight, Uncle Morris drove us to Idlewild Airport. We held our tickets and went with the Greenes to board the plane. Aunt Bea, Aunt Blanche, and Uncle Morris, stood outside behind a chain link fence and waved good-bye to us as we ascended the tall staircase that led to the entrance of the aircraft. Two pretty stewardesses in crisp uniforms and hats, showed the way to our seats. They gave us gum and told us to chew it to minimize the pressure when the propeller jet took off. The pilot gave my brother a pair of wings and allowed Danny, Marla, and me into the cabin to see all of the instruments the pilot and co-pilot used in flight. He reassured us that flying was great and we would like it. We sat down next to Marla and her parents and were thrilled to be in an airplane for the very first time. We loved the flight. Marla was not so happy. She was throwing up into the vomit bag provided in the pocket of the seat in front of her. Danny and I tried to ignore the vomiting and he said to me," Yup, our parents were right. This is going to be a big adventure going to California."

Chapter Nine
Our First Introduction to Life in L.A.:
1955 – 1958

Uncle Sam drove to the airport to pick us up in his Buick. I remember that car so well. It was a shiny light-blue vehicle with massive chrome bumpers front and back and three distinctive chrome circles on the driver's side near the Buick logo. It was the most luxurious car my brother, Danny, and I ever rode in, with very plushy cloth, comfortable seats and air conditioning, an option that was too expensive for our dad to have in our plain, no frills station wagon. We sat in the back seat with our cousin, Bonnie, who was a year older than my brother. She was ten and quite precocious. She told her parents, Sam and Shirley where we would like to have lunch. "Rozzie and Danny have never been to a drive-in. Let's go to Bob's Big Boy."

We were very excited to eat at a drive-in. We didn't have them at home in New York. We had only seen these outdoor restaurants in Hollywood movies. It was really a treat for us. Uncle Sam pulled his Buick up to a spot in the parking lot and a carhop approached. She was wearing a red hat with elastic to hold it under her chin, a red jacket with brass buttons and a pair of black satin shorts. On her feet she had white roller skates and was carrying a tray. She took our order of burgers, sodas and fries, and skated to a window to put in the order. It was a fun experience for us New York kids to have lunch at a California drive-in. Our mother would not have approved of us eating such unhealthy food if she were with us.

Years later when we returned to L.A. with our own children to visit the family, I asked my cousin Bob if we could go back to that same Bob's Big Boy. We did, but it was no longer a drive-in, just a regular hamburger restaurant. But it did have the original statue in front of a big boy holding a hamburger in his hand. The next week vandals stole the famous statue and the police were searching for it. What a shame. Such an iconic symbol of the 1950s and it was gone.

Chapter Ten
A New Life

In California where we moved with our parents in 1955, our grandfather Morris owned the apartment building where we lived. Our Uncle Sam, Aunt Shirley, and their daughter, Bonnie had an apartment on the third floor near ours and our grandparents were on the first floor. Also, we had aunts, uncles, and cousins nearby. Uncle Lou and Aunt Corinne had two daughters, Andrea and Debbie. Uncle Harry and Aunt Sara had a daughter, Francine, and a son, our cousin Bob. On the weekends, the family assembled in someone's home, usually Aunt Sara's since she had the biggest one.

My grandparents, Morris and Rose, spoke with thick Jewish accents and pinched our cheeks until we howled. To us American-born children, they were very exotic. "Vat's nu, dahlink?" my grandma asked me in her heavy accent. It was a ritual to have Sunday night dinner with our grandparents in their apartment. Grandpa and

Grandma drank hot tea out of glasses. Grandma asked us if we wanted any, but we only drank tea if we were sick and so, declined the offer. They also had Borscht or Schav, cold beet soups that they asked us to eat, but we said no. The main course was boiled chicken and potatoes, sometimes chicken soup with matzoh balls or little chicken eggs in it and for dessert, Grandma's home-made sugar cookies. "No cookies, Rozzie and Danny unless you eat the food," our grandfather admonished us.

After the meal, we sat on the couch with our grandma who loved watching *Gorgeous George* on the television or *Roller Derby* if that program was on. At eight o'clock on Sunday night, Grandma announced, "Max Solomon (her version of Ed Sullivan) is on." Grandma gave him a Jewish name since he had a Jewish wife and she was convinced he was Jewish too.

Our grandparents appeared to be ancient to Danny and me. Our grandfather had a receding hairline with white curly hair and slate blue eyes like our dad's. He often dressed in all white, a starched white short-sleeved shirt tucked into pressed cuffed white pants, and white shoes. Grandma was very tiny, only four feet ten inches with dark olive skin, a long hooked nose, and short wavy, pepper and salt hair. She wore baggy dresses, black orthopedic shoes, stockings rolled up over her knees, and she had gold filigree earrings in her pierced ears. She resembled a Gypsy woman to our young eyes. None of the American ladies we saw in Los Angeles had pierced ears or wore dangling earrings. The style was clip-on earrings like Doris Day wore in the movies. Grandma had a taciturn expression unlike her jovial husband who was always smiling and teasing his grandchildren.

One day Grandpa took us for a walk around the neighborhood and on the way home, we followed him to the back of the building where there was a cement parking lot. He reached up where tree branches were overhanging a cement wall and plucked something off the trees. "What are you doing, Grandpa?" Danny asked.

"These are almonds. Let me break open some and you can taste them," he said. As we were eating the nuts, Grandpa continued speaking. "When I was a little boy in Romania and about your age, Danny, I used to go into a farmer's field and climb up into his almond trees to get the nuts. One day the farmer caught me, made me climb down from the tree and he pinched my ear. 'Thief, don't steal my almonds,' he told me, 'or I will go to your parents and make them pay for what you stole.' I, of course, didn't want him to tell my parents and asked what I could do to help him on the farm. 'Come here, boy, to the barn.' He walked me into the barn and showed me how to pitch hay into bundles for his horses and mules. I spent a few hours making bundles of hay for the farmer until he let me go home. I ran home and learned my lesson well. I never climbed into his orchard again."

"But, what about these trees, Grandpa?" I asked.

"These are my almond trees that I planted on my property. So, we can have as many almonds as we want, *shaina maidele.*" My Grandpa called me his "pretty little girl" in the Yiddish language.

That afternoon my brother and I learned about our grandfather's boyhood in Europe. It was hard for us to imagine that our grandpa had once been a child.

Chapter Eleven

Meeting Our Cousins

July of 1955 was a big adjustment for my brother and me. Our parents drove to California and we flew there with people who were also moving to California. We were staying with grandparents we barely knew and waiting for our parents to arrive. We were going to stay with our grandparents until our parents came and we all moved into apartment 3C in Grandpa's building. "We need to buy furniture and set up an apartment," Daddy explained. They bought beds, night tables, dressers for their rooms and beds, dressers, and desks for our rooms. Our parents chose a couch, coffee table, lamps, a dinette table, and four chairs for the kitchen and living room.

Daddy's favorite piece of furniture was the red canvas chair he bought at a discount store called the Akron, the '50s version of Target. It was his T.V. chair and only he sat in it.

There was still time before we had to register for school in September and we were bored just playing by ourselves. Our cousin, Bonnie, was busy with her friends at camp and only saw us on weekends. Our parents promised to take us to meet more of our cousins at Aunt Sara's house. "When can we go to Aunt Sara's?" Danny and I asked. "As soon as we're all settled, we'll go," Daddy promised us.

On a hot Sunday afternoon, Pop told us there was a family gathering at Aunt Sara's and our Aunt Corinne, Uncle Lou, and their daughters, Andrea and Debbie, would be there too. Danny and I were very happy to have kids to play with.

We arrived at four and went through the gate to the backyard pool area. Our aunts and uncles kissed us and Aunt Sara asked," Are you hungry, kids?" Of course, our answer was yes and we were allowed to have some soft drinks and chips before the barbecue would be served later. "Don't eat a lot because you'll want to swim in the pool before the meal is served at about five thirty."

Danny and I had our first introduction to our cousin, Fran, Sara's daughter, a 14-year-old obnoxious teenager. She was very tall, extremely heavy, and mischievous. She loved animals and had a collie named Tara that followed her around the yard and a cat that had given birth to five kittens. We were horrified when she threw the kittens into the pool. "Oh no," we shouted. "They'll drown!" "Don't worry," she told us. "It's their natural instinct to swim." They did swim and she scooped each one out of the pool and allowed them to return to their mother. "Why don't you come into the pool?" she asked us. We had our suits under our clothes and were glad to oblige. Francine was gentle with Danny and me in the pool, but very rough with her younger brother, Bob. She kept dunking him under water. He retaliated by splashing her, but we feared for his life every time she grabbed him and threw him underwater. Aunt Sara witnessed the antics and made Francine come out of the pool. "Children, go upstairs and change into your dry clothes." We were glad to be away from Francine for a while. She could be mean. While I was in the pool she teased me by saying, "We don't swim in your toilet, so please don't pee in our pool." I answered her, "I'm not a baby. I'm not gonna pee in the pool!"

Aunt Sara had a live-in maid who helped serve the hamburgers, frankfurters, and salads. We learned later that Margaret quit her job with Aunt Sara and joined a female singing group that made a record and had some success.

When we finished eating, the children were permitted to go into the den and play or watch T.V. Francine had an idea for all of us that we liked. She was going to dress the girls in kimonos Aunt Sara had from a trip to Japan a few years ago. She had written a skit called "Little Leechee Nut" based on the Three Bears story and she was going to have us act it out with pantomime and she would film us with her dad's movie camera. The three little girls, Andrea, nine, me, seven, and her sister Debbie, five, were little Chinese girls lost in the woods. My cousin, Bob, was the woodman and my brother Danny, was the wolf a role he loved because he could scare us. Francine had a Halloween mask of a wolf for Danny and a plaid shirt and jeans for Bob. We wore the kimonos pinned up to make them smaller and Fran had make-up left over from Halloween that she used to paint our faces. Since it was a silent movie, Fran showed us how to pantomime the story in a very exaggerated way. When we were done Francine had the film developed and on another visit to her house, all of the relatives viewed the movie in the den. They, of course, loved it. We were in Hollywood after all!

Chapter Twelve
Summer Is Ending

Summer was winding down and soon our mother was going to register us in the local school, Lankershim Elementary. While we were still on vacation, our parents discovered a park near where we lived. They had a recreation program, but it was too late to sign us up this summer. Pop said we could go to their summer program the next year. This summer, he promised me to teach me how to ride a two-wheel bicycle and one hot August afternoon late in the day when the sun wasn't as brutal, he took me to the park by myself. He held onto the back of the bicycle seat running as I rode and saying to me, "Keep pedaling. I won't let go." Of course, in a few minutes he did take his hands away and I was riding free. I fell off, but he convinced me to try again and in a short while, I was balancing and riding the bike very well. "Wow, I can't wait to tell Danny and Mommy when we get home that I can ride my two-wheeler." "It's great. Now we can ride as a family," Pop told me. My parents didn't buy bikes in California and his prediction never came true. Nevertheless, I was thrilled to learn this new skill that you never forget.

One day before August ended, my parents allowed Danny and me to walk to Lankershim Park with our cousin, Bonnie. They gave us pocket money to spend and we went to a small candy store to buy little miniature cream pies, candy, and soda. "Let's have our candy at this picnic table under a leafy shade tree," Danny suggested to us girls. Bonnie did not sit down. She saw a few boys and ran towards them to flirt with the older guys. She was a very pretty 10-year-old child with dark curly hair, bright hazel eyes, and long eyelashes. She had a slim build and when she laughed, you saw her dimples in each cheek. The 12-year-old boys were captivated by Bonnie and reluctantly parted ways when their dad came to pick them up. "Let's have our goodies," I called out to Bonnie and Danny who were on the swings. "Okay," Bonnie yelled to her younger, quieter cousin. We sat down on the bench at the picnic table, sipped our soft drinks, and began to unwrap our creamy desserts. Bonnie took hers and threw it at us. She thought it was funny to throw a cream pie at us, but Danny and I were upset. "Hey. If you don't want to eat your pie and candy it doesn't matter, but we do!" Danny chased Bonnie around the table. It was attention she wanted. I ate my pie in silence and saved Danny's dessert for later.

Danny looked at his watch. "It's three-thirty and our parents want us back by four. We have to leave the park right now." Bonnie ran ahead and we followed her. When we were home in our apartment, we complained about Bonnie's wild behavior. Mom and Pop agreed that she was not an appropriate role model for us and we were not permitted to be alone again with our cousin.

Bonnie didn't improve with age. She became more unruly and rebellious. Her mother Shirley was not a disciplinarian and did not supervise her daughter enough. She had her own dress shop and spent long hours there. Bonnie's step-father, Sam, worked in his real estate office until seven or eight in the evening and also worked weekends. Bonnie resented her step-dad, my Uncle Sam, and longed to see her biological father, Shirley's first husband. I don't think he saw her much nor did he pay child support very well. Sam was supporting Bonnie and doing the best he knew how to be her father. Bonnie ran with a rough crowd in high school. She was disinterested in studying and Shirley and Sam hoped she would find a husband and get married. They were not aware that their beautiful girl was drinking heavily, partying, and skipping classes. After high school, Bonnie was experimenting with drugs and eventually became a heroine addict. For years, Shirley and Sam suffered as Bonnie declined more and more. Sam went to flop houses in seedy sections of L.A. to retrieve Bonnie and bring her to a hospital. After years of abuse, she finally completed a rehabilitation program and was clean. But, she had ruined her health and needed open heart surgery to repair damage to her heart valves. When I was in my 20s and visiting the family in California, my fiancé and I had dinner with Bonnie and her parents. I was astonished by her appearance. The lovely young girl I remembered looked older than her years. She did have a secretarial position in an insurance company and an apartment that her parents provided. When we returned to my cousin Bob's house and were alone in our room, I commented to the man who was going to be my husband, "Our children will not be like Bonnie or Francine, my other troubled cousin." "No way," Scott agreed with me.

Chapter Thirteen
Starting School

Before the last day in August, our mom walked us to Lankershim Elementary School to register us for the coming year. I was entering the third grade and my brother would be in a fourth grade class. "Good luck," the school secretary wished us. "You'll like Lankershim. All the kids do." "Thank you," we replied and then headed home to Magnolia Boulevard just two blocks away from the school. We were going to walk to school with our cousin, Bonnie, and other children in the building.

The first day of school was awkward. I was very shy with children I didn't know, but the teacher was kind and smiled a lot and the classmates were friendly. Danny liked his fourth grade teacher, but was unhappy. She gave him homework. "Aw gee. We have to read a story in the text book she handed out." "Oh, maybe you can read me the story," I told him. At three we waited outside to walk home with Bonnie, Barbie, a neighbor's daughter, and Jack Olson, a sixth grader who was in his last year of the school. Mommy was waiting for us to hear about our school experiences. "I baked chocolate chip cookies for you. And take some milk." "I have homework," Danny groaned. "What is it?" our mother asked us. "I have to read a five-page story." "Well," our mother said to us. "Go outside to play for an hour and then, you can do your reading." Our parents believed in playtime before we did our work. "Dinner is at six when your father comes home."

We adjusted to the educational system in California. It was quite different from our school in New York. At recess we were outside all the time unless it rained which it seldom did. We spent more time inside our classroom when we were in Laurelton. In L.A. we learned how to play tetherball and our teachers taught us to square dance, another western custom. We ate lunch at picnic tables under a covered awning. Sometimes we had the school lunch or brought bagged sandwiches from home. It was the first time Danny and I had Spam luncheon meat, a popular item on the menu. We thought it was odd food and avoided it when we discovered it was mystery meat. Reading and math were the same in L.A. Mission History was unique to California schools. We learned about the friars who established churches in San Juan Capistrano and other locales. The school resembled a mission building with its white stucco walls and red tiled roof.

Halloween was a lot of fun. We were going to be in a school play and were invited to parties where we were going to bob for apples. We went trick or treating in our neighborhood. I dressed up as a princess and my brother was a ghoul. Our mother put grease makeup on our faces and Pop accompanied us and other neighborhood children to houses on the block. In New York, we had to wear heavy coats on an October evening, but here, we put on light jackets or sweaters over our costumes.

In May, the school was going to celebrate May Day with a big pageant and Danny was going to be a star in a school play. He dressed in a medieval costume, a big hat with a plume, and embroidered coat. He carried a large scroll and was going to read a proclamation to the King and his subjects. The girls were going to dance around the Maypoles that were decorated with colorful ribbons. "I love this day," I told our mother. "I want to wear my pink dress with the purple polka dots that you made for me."

School ended well that first year in Los Angeles. We made friends with some of the children in our classes and as promised, Mommy was enrolling us in the summer program in Lankershim Park. It was an arts and crafts program for two hours daily. Danny and I loved our counselor, Miss Delaney, a very statuesque, attractive lady with creamy white skin, long auburn hair she wore in a braid down her back, and the most gorgeous green eyes. She taught us how to roll out clay and make it into myriad shapes that we were going to glaze. We made platters out of white clay and when they were fired, we held screens over them and splattered color on the ceramic pieces. I used a green glaze and Danny chose blue. Another project was an angel for the girls and an animal for the boys. The angel was made with a pattern that each girl placed on the clay and cut out. Danny made a whale and I still have it in a drawer in my kitchen. I loved making the ceramic projects, but was less successful in making lanyards. Our mother made a fuss over whatever we brought home from camp and she used our platters and we wore our lanyards with the ceramic slides on our shirts.

While we were occupied at the recreation center, our mother did her artwork. She was somewhat bored and lonely. She didn't have women friends to play Mah Jong with or talk to as she had when we lived in Laurelton. We sensed that Mommy missed her sisters and friends in New York.

One day, our mother found a little grey and white kitten in front of the apartment building and brought the stray home. "Can we keep her?" We begged Pop who made all of the family decisions. After pleading steadily, he relented and let us keep her. "What do you want to name the kitten?" Mommy asked us. "She has white boots like the Puss 'N Boots story my teacher, Miss Nichols, read to us," I said. "How about Bootsie?" my brother suggested. We all loved that name for her. She grew up to be a regal beauty. She had long hair and big, round yellow eyes. Bootsie sat like a queen on the windowsill and gazed out the window at people and animals passing by. Our mother painted a portrait of her in oil. I think I have it somewhere in my garage.

We enjoyed the summer program immensely and asked our parents if we could go back the following year especially if Miss Delaney was going to work there again.

Chapter fourteen

Back to Our Roots

One evening in 1958, after we were living in North Hollywood for three years, we noticed a change in our parents. They were unusually quiet. And our dad was never silent. He usually talked a lot and ruled the roost. We were wondering why they weren't asking us about our day after Pop sat on his red chair and read the paper in the living room and shushed us to hear the six o'clock news while we were eating dinner in the dinette. My brother gave me a non-verbal nod to ask, "What's up?"

Finally, Pop ushered us into the living room and we sat next to Mom and Bootsie, the cat. He began to tell us about a new parental decision.

"Your mother and I have been talking about going back to New York," he said.

"What?" my brother Danny piped up from his comfortable spot on the sofa next to our mother who was holding a purring kitty on her lap.

"Why?" I whined on my seat adjacent to my older brother. "I don't want to leave Grandma and Grandpa and my friends. No, I won't move again. You can't make me." My voice rose and tears spilled from my eyes.

Danny was more stoic, but he did not accept what our father was telling us either.

Pop tried to reason with us. "There's a recession in California and it's very hard for me to make a living. If I don't go back to New York, I'll lose my teaching license. Your mother and I agreed to try living here for three years and if it didn't work out, I could still get my teaching job back at Far Rockaway High."

I had no idea what a recession was, but I did know our father had to work to support our family.

Danny tried to convince Pop that one of his brothers would give him a job, but the truth was that none of the three brothers worked well with other people. Their personalities were just too strong. And being a teacher was the perfect profession for Pop. He had a captive, receptive audience at Far Rockaway. They hung onto every intelligent word he uttered.

Our mother was also going to be happier in New York. She had her two sisters there and she was in love with the art culture in New York City. L.A. in the '50s was a vast wasteland devoid of culture. There were few museums or art classes.

We ran to our rooms. I was sobbing on my pillow. Danny sat at his desk in his bedroom and assembled a plastic car model of a '57 T-Bird. He hated to leave his school friends and cousins behind. He had bonded with his cousin, Bob, who was about the same age, height, and physical size. Bob liked visiting our apartment and escaping his bullying, harassing, teenage sister. Aunt Sara was content to drop him off with us and go to her girlfriends' card games. Her favorite game was Pam, popular with the wealthy ladies of Beverly Hills.

Danny brought his metallic blue model into my room to show me. "Like it?" he asked me. I was on the floor playing with my bride doll, putting on her plastic high heels and her veil. "Yeah, it's cool."

We sat and talked about everything we experienced living in California.

"Remember the snail races we had outside the building our first summer here?"

"Before we made friends, we did a lot of stuff like that", I recalled. "We also met our next-door neighbor who made miniature sets for movies. He let us pick up the trains and tiny people he was painting and he explained how the photographers make them look bigger on film."

"He was really nice."

"Uh huh." We were both lying down on the carpeted floor with our hands holding up our heads and kicking out our legs behind us.

"I'm going to miss my friends, Barbara and Deena." I smiled as I thought of each girl. I met Barbara on the playground at school the first day of my second year. She was picking her nose and didn't try to hide it and I once had the same habit, but was reprimanded by Aunt Shirley who stopped me from continuing my habit. Barbara was very tiny and had dark curly hair. We were friends in fourth grade. My good friend in fifth grade was Deena, a very pretty girl with light-brown braided hair, green eyes, and hanging earrings like my grandmother had. "Why do you wear those earrings?" I asked her. "My mother is part Cherokee and she had my ears pierced when I was a baby. She gave me this pair when I turned nine," she explained. I was taller and chubbier than both girls or "solid" as my father described me. I admired the thin kids.

Danny was in a nostalgic mood. "Remember the time our neighbor, Barbie, and her parents went away for the weekend and we took care of their talking parakeet?"

"The bird kept asking, "Where's Barbie?" We thought

he was so smart, but our mother said he repeated everything his family said. There were other expressions he repeated dozens of times, but we didn't remember them.

Danny had a lot of school buddies, but most of all he wanted to be with our cousin, Bob. I too preferred seeing our cousins Bob, Andrea, and Debbie.

We didn't like Francine or Bonnie too much. The older girls had problems that grew with their ages. I don't even know where Francine is today and sadly, Bonnie died about a year ago. Today, I maintain a good relationship with Bob, Debbie, and their families. I am trying to become reacquainted with Andrea, but she remains aloof.

My brother and I recalled a funny incident involving Aunt Sara and Uncle Harry. They went to Las Vegas on vacation and saw some of the headliner shows. Aunt Sara happened to catch Elvis after performing and asked for his autograph. A photographer snapped their photo and Aunt Sara and Elvis Presley appeared on a teen magazine a little while afterwards. Francine, who bought that magazine regularly, screamed when she saw her mother and Elvis on the cover.

"Mother, how did you get that picture with Elvis?" Sara related the story to Fran about the man who took her picture when she asked Elvis for an autograph.

Danny and I listened to some of Elvis' songs like *Blue Suede Shoes* and *Hound Dog*. But, I thought Elvis was "greasy" and didn't go gaga over him like my cousin did. Silly when I think about it. We preferred quirky songs like *Flying Purple Eater*. We played it over and over until the 45 skipped.

There was one sad event that happened and disturbed us a lot.

"I'll never forget about the plane that crashed in a schoolyard and killed a lot of children." We secretly believed we could have been the casualties even though it didn't happen at our school.

"I hope we don't fly back to New York," Danny commented.

"No, we're driving to New York."

Mom and Pop entered the room and said it was late.

"Lights out, kids,"

Pop no longer read us bedtime stories. We were too big, but a story tonight would have been comforting.

We kissed our parents and Danny went to his room to finish a chapter in his English reader.

An era was coming to an end. In a few short months we would have to give up our cat, Bootsie, to a neighbor who owned a ranch out in the valley and kiss our grandparents and all of our aunts, uncles, and cousins goodbye.

51

Chapter Fifteen
A Tug of Emotions Saying Goodbye

The bad thing about being a child is that your parents don't consider your feelings when they make decisions that affect you. Pop was the ultimate authority and Mom obeyed blindly except when one of his ideas negatively impacted her life. I remember only two such occasions when she dared to say no to him. Once was when he wanted to buy and manage a run-down hotel in the Catskills. My mom knew she would have to do three quarters of the physical work while he supervised. She wisely refused. We were surprised again by the second argument she won. Pop bragged about her art talent to a gallery owner and badgered the man to show mom's work. She was very upset by his behavior, took him aside, and berated him. "Don't push me to exhibit if I don't want to. It's clear the man doesn't want to see my watercolors and you embarrassed me." Our mother battled Pop over her issues, but never took our side against him. Despite his meanness, she never defended us. Parents should present a united front, but there are moments when a parent has to recognize a mistake made by another. I never forgave my father for calling me "retarded." His cruel words stung forever.

We looked to see what our mother would say when Pop announced we were going back to New York. We had been living in L.A. for three years and we were happy living in Grandpa's apartment's building. I looked at Mom's face. She sat impassively while Pop explained his plan for the family. Danny took Bootsie and stoically walked to his room. I ran sobbing to mine. I threw myself down on the bed and cried so many tears that my pillow became a soggy, wrinkled mass of cotton and foam rubber. I thought about my grandparents who lived in the apartment below ours. We loved our dinners with them every Sunday, walks around the neighborhood with Grandpa Morris and his stories. I cried about leaving our relatives and our pet. I didn't fall asleep until I really tired myself out emotionally with a lot of heartache.

The next day, Saturday, our parents offered us lunch at Bob's Big Boy, the first restaurant we went to with Uncle

Sam, Aunt Shirley, and Bonnie. We had sullen faces, but accepted their proposal.

"You'll see Aunt Bea, Uncle Morris, Aunt Blanche, and your new uncle, Irv, when we return to New York."

"But, we are going to miss our grandparents," Danny exclaimed. "How often will they come to New York or we to California?"

"We have to make new friends and change schools."

"We have to give up Bootsie," we both cried.

"That's true, but Bootsie will have a new home and you'll get used to a new school and will make new friends."

I thought it was easy for him to say. He doesn't have many friends here nor does Mom.

Pop drove up to the burger joint. We went in and sat in a booth near the window. Neither our mother nor our father restrained us from ordering large burgers, fries, or ice cream.

"Your eyes are bigger than your stomachs," was the only comment Mom made to chubby 10-year-old me.

She was right. I ate too much and needed Alka Seltzer when we reached home. Danny was unaffected by the food since he was older and eating like a pre-teen.

That night my brother and I played checkers in his room, Bootsie at our side poking the pieces around with her paws. We both tolerated the cat interrupting our game and he let me win. We discussed our plight and became resigned to it. Danny explained we could use the situation for leverage. I realized what he meant. If they felt sorry for us, we could ask for privileges or things they ordinarily wouldn't let us have. Our parents' philosophy was that children should be seen and not heard, but when they looked at our despondent faces, they would be more sympathetic towards us.

Chapter Sixteen

Sunrise, a New Beginning

The car was totally packed with all of our clothing in suitcases and the camping gear—a tent, Coleman stove, lanterns, thermal food bag, and a large metal thermos. Our apartment was emptied out days ago and we stayed with Aunt Shirley, Uncle Sam, and our grandparents. We stayed in Uncle Sam's place and shared the bedroom with Bonnie. We were designated a number of toys we were allowed to bring in the car. I had two dolls: my small ballerina and one with black hair and moveable eyes. Danny had fifteen comic books fastened with an elastic band and a metal airplane he liked the best of his models. He had outgrown the toy ham radio set and gave it to a friend in the building. Today we were going to say goodbye to Grandpa Morris and Grandma Rose and neighbors from the building that were driving back to Connecticut in the next few days. Grandma and Grandpa made us lunch yesterday and we even deigned to drink Grandma's hot tea from glasses. Grandma cried a little and said to her son, "Oy, Solly. Do you have to go back to New York?" He patted her arm softly and responded, "My teaching job is waiting for me there. Sorry, Mom." The next morning very early we went outside and took some photos with the Buchannans, the people on our floor who were leaving California and returning to their hometown and awaiting family. We took all our family photos the night before at dinner with the relatives in a restaurant. Uncle Sam, the most prosperous Schindler brother, paid for everyone.

The neighbors were up early to pack for their departure also, so we asked them to pose for a last photograph in front of the building. They asked us in for breakfast, but Pop declined, telling them we'd eat on the road. By seven a.m., we waved our last goodbye and were starting out on the highways that existed back then, before freeways completely took over in Los Angeles. As a matter of fact, a freeway was built on the site where our building was torn down many years later. It was hard for my brother and me to see a vacant space on Magnolia Boulevard where we used to live when we went back to L.A. as teenagers. Grandma and Grandpa were gone by then. California had long ago ceased to be our home. But, we had good memories and traveled more easily in a newer station wagon on roads that were much improved since the old ones of the '50s.

It took longer at that time to crisscross the country and drive to New York, but our dad had his route mapped out carefully way in advance of that hot morning we left L.A. Mom held the map and navigated as she had been instructed. Our first big destination was going to be Yosemite National Park and we were going to camp out in the woods. Pop showed us the maps and explained how he and our mother were going to drive from west to east, avoiding some of the states in the deep south that were not safe for Jews to be in. We were in the same tenuous position as Negroes—not accepted by the white, narrow-minded population in those segregated areas.

Danny asked," What's wrong with passing through Little Rock, Arkansas?"

"Negroes are not allowed in white restaurants or businesses. They drink from separate water fountains and use separate bathrooms. Jews have to be careful also and steer clear of some of the rough white folks who do not like us. The Klu Klux Klan is very dangerous and hates everyone who is unlike them."

"I don't understand," I said.

"There's no way to understand this hatred, but it

exists," Mom told me.

After that discussion, Danny and I were eerily quiet in the back seat of our old station wagon. He read a Superman comic and I took out a new outfit for my doll from her little case and changed her dress. After two hours, we fell asleep and didn't awake until Pop pulled into a gas station to fill up and let Mom spell him by taking the wheel for an hour or more. Danny and I had some leverage with Pop in terms of getting more privileges because we had lamented the loss of Bootsie, our beloved cat, who had to live on farm in California and not go back with us to New York. So, we tried out our first request on Pop.

"We know you don't like us to have a lot of soda, but it's so hot and nothing else will quench our thirst as well," Danny said and I nodded my agreement.

"All right. Take a coke from the icebox inside the gas station." Pop still referred to a fridge as an icebox, a holdover from his youth before there was refrigeration.

"How about an ice cream too?" I asked my mother who was mopping her brow with an embroidered hankie.

"You're pushing your luck, Rozzie. It's not even lunchtime yet. We'll stop in two hours at a picnic spot and have the sandwiches I prepared. Tonight we can buy ice cream."

She glanced at my crestfallen face and said to both of us, "Go into the car. It's time to get on the road and drive more distance." Pop had finished getting gas, paid the attendant, and we were off again. This time, we drove three hours until we stopped. We picnicked near a lake and Pop told us we could put our feet in and cool off from the extreme heat. He parked under a tree, but without air-conditioning in the car, only the breeze of the open windows was better than we were at a light and it was boiling in the car. Mom drove until it was later on in the afternoon and not as hot. We drove into a large town and sought out a motel with a vacancy sign. Pop went into the office to ask about the price of a room for the night. When we saw him exit the front of the motel, we knew we would have to drive on and locate a cheaper place. Ten minutes later, we parked in a shady place, Pop came out of the office with a key and we settled in for the night.

"What about dinner?" we asked.

"Mom is too tired to make us anything so we'll eat at that café we passed down the road. We can even walk there."

Danny and I made faces about walking and Pop agreed to take the car to the restaurant. They had hamburgers, but it was nothing like Bob's Big Boy in L.A. It was just a Mom and Pop establishment. Our mother suggested chicken for all of us and we reluctantly accepted rather than burgers and fries. But, she did promise ice cream. So, we were okay and we all ate hungrily. Pop had chocolate ice cream and Danny and I chose flavors we liked—he had chocolate chip and I had strawberry. Mom didn't have any. She often refrained from sweets because she was somewhat overweight as many mothers were in the '50s. After the meal, we listened to Pop's storytelling and his explanation of where we were going tomorrow and what sights we would see. Danny and I were excited about sightseeing—usually that meant souvenirs. We didn't complain when Pop told us all, "Lights out." We would have to get up early and start driving so we could be in Yosemite before dark. That night we all fell asleep fast and were well rested for the next day's journey. Since we all slept in the same room, Danny and I couldn't talk about how we would use our powers of persuasion to get souvenirs, but we had prearranged hand signs to indicate that we'd team up to wheedle new stuff from Pop. We had the light on for an extra minute and did the special kid signs and then turned out the lamp and went to sleep. I dreamed about Bootsie chasing chickens on the farm

and then taking a nap in the barn on a straw bed. I'd tell
Danny about my dream tomorrow.

62

Chapter Seventeen

Back on the Road

The alarm clock's shrill sound aroused us from our cots and our parents from their double bed. Mom and Pop took the first showers and they cautioned us to wash ourselves well when it was our turns so we could skip the showers at the campground the next night. We promised to use the washcloths provided by the motel. I took along an extra one for my dolls and tucked it into my dress pocket, the red one I would wear on the trip to Yosemite that was identical to my mom's sundress. Mom said we would have to wear pedal pushers when we camped. She was going to have me watch her do laundry at the campground's facility while Pop and Danny pitched the tent at our campsite.

"Mom, how long are we going to be in Yosemite?" I asked when we all had showers and were leaving the room to get breakfast at the motel's dining room. She said, "Two days."

The motel's restaurant had a special: kids under12 eat free. Pop (usually an honest Abe) told Danny to say he was 11 even though he was already 12.

"Rozzie, don't give away Danny's real age, please," Mom said to me because I was frowning at Pop's lack of honesty.

"But, Pop says to tell the truth."

"There are a few exceptions to the rule, Rozzie, "Pop said sternly.

Danny and I had pancakes because we were averse to eating runny eggs. Mom and Pop ordered the eggs with ham and toast. I put jelly on the pancakes because I didn't care much for syrup on pancakes. Danny convinced Mom to let us order chocolate milk. The waitress called us, "Sugar," and brought us pretty big glasses of the heavenly elixir. Mom kept her negative opinion of the beverages to herself and Pop tasted Danny's chocolate milk much to my brother's chagrin. What kid wants a starving parent eating or drinking what is theirs? Mom advised us to use the restrooms and it was time to pay the check and go. Danny asked Pop for postcards from the rack outside the motel office and bought 10 for 50 cents.

"You can write the family and friends, kids," he told us as he started the car's ignition. The wagon sputtered and off we were again on the road.

Danny and I chose our cards and we began writing. I wrote to my cousins, Debbie and Andrea first:

> "Dear cusins,
>   We had choclat milk. Pop is driving us to Yosemite.
>   Love,
>   Roz"

My spelling wasn't perfect. I planned to ask Mom to correct my cards when we were in the park later today. Danny chose to write our cousins, Francine and Bob, with his first postcard. Writing and napping kept us occupied until Pop made his first pit stop. What we didn't realize at first was the necessity for Pop to stop the car sooner than he planned. As we awoke, we heard a loud hissing sound and Pop said, "Damn." He never cursed so we were concerned.

"What's going on, Saul?" Mom opened her eyes and questioned what the problem was.

"The hood of the car is smoking," Danny cried out.

A scruffy mechanic wearing torn denim overalls, an anchor tattoo, and a tee shirt rolled up with a cigarette pack tucked under one short sleeve, approached and casually addressed Pop,

"Problem, Mister?"

"It looks that way. What'll it cost for you to look under the hood and fix what's broken?"

"Mebbe a few bucks or can be more, if you need parts," he told our dad who had little choice. The next stop was 20 miles from this tumbleweed town.

"You can sit on this here bench with your family, Mister, while I look at the radiator."

Danny and I were restless and started swatting each other with paper fans they gave us at the gas station. Our parents warned us to behave or, "No desserts for you tonight and you'll go to bed earlier." We calmed down, but when one hour stretched into two, we were grumpy and ill-mannered again. Pop said, "They had to get a part from some distance away and are just now fixing the car."

"Kids, go get drinks and ice cream from the Esso Station. Here's two dollars." We argued about who was holding the money, but were content to buy treats.

When we came back, Pop was smiling. The repair was reasonable. Mom was not as happy because the delay meant we weren't reaching Yosemite until late in the evening.

They took turns driving and we saved time by eating sandwiches in the car under a tree rather than finding a picnic area. Danny and I played word games naming cars on the road we spotted alphabetically, and reading, writing, and napping.

Restaurants were scarce in the area close to Yosemite, but Pop asked in the tourist office on the side of the road where to locate a reasonably priced one.

"Up there two hundred yards is Dolly's."

Our tired parents were in a weakened state of mind and didn't object to us ordering burgers and fries. Even Mom ate some of the French fries and decided to have a small dish of vanilla ice cream.

"Only five more miles to the entrance of Yosemite Park," Pop said when we were back in the car.

"Estelle, get the flashlight out of the glove compartment. I'll need it to pitch our tent."

We went to our campsite, directed by the ranger at the gate and a really kind stranger in the adjoining campsite helped Pop set up our tent while the rest of us sat on folding chairs watching the whole process. Two boys came out of their tent to play with us.

"Remember to keep your food well secured and hidden in your car," the nice camping neighbor advised us. The bears scavenge at all hours."

I heard the word "bears" and I was petrified they'd break into our tent. My eyes were big as saucers.

Mom calmed my fears. "There's no food in our tent, so they won't bother us. Don't worry."

We used flashlights, one for each of us, to walk the path to the bathrooms.

"Wash up and brush your teeth, kids. We'll shower in the morning."

Tomorrow was going to be fun. Pop said the rangers were giving a talk about the park after breakfast and there was a guided hike. We hoped the boys in the tent next to us were going with their parents. Mom and Pop told us to quiet down and sleep. They were on their folding cots and we were snuggled in our sleeping bags on the tent's cloth floor.

"Good night, Mom and Pop."

"Go to sleep, Rozzie and Danny."

We fell asleep quickly and didn't hear our father's horrific snoring.

Chapter Eighteen
In Yosemite Park

Daylight was streaming into the tent by seven in the morning. We gathered our clothes, soaps, and washcloths, and made our way in our pajamas and robes to the shower area. The men went to their building and my mother and I walked to the women's showers.

Back at our campsite, Mom set up the Coleman stove on the station wagon tailgate.

"What are you making for breakfast?" my hungry brother was asking.

"Scrambled eggs and some toast, instant coffee for us, and juice or milk for you and Rozzie."

We smelled the aroma of bacon on the cookstove our neighbor was using. She was frying up bacon and eggs. Her two boys were also eating Wonder bread and drinking chocolate Yoo-Hoo from the containers. Our mother did not buy white bread or bacon and didn't allow us to drink sweetened milk either.

Mrs. Petersen offered us chocolate chip cookies, but Mom gave us a look of disapproval and we declined them.

Danny asked Owen, one of their sons, "Are you going to the Ranger Talk at nine?"

"Yup. Want to walk together?"

"Yeah."

So, the four adults walked in front down the path to the seating area and we four children followed in back of them.

"Look, a mother bear and her cub," Owen shouted to his father, Jim. It was a short distance from us."

"We'll take the other trail to the Ranger Talk and leave the animals alone," Pop advised us.

Sure enough, the ranger said to keep a safe distance from the bears. He warned everyone again about the dangers the bears posed.

"Never keep food in your tent. Make sure it's in an insulated icebox in your car. Throw all garbage into the secure cans provided at your campsites. Extinguish all fires completely."

He spoke about hiking trails, waterfalls, trees, plants, and the wild animals that inhabit the park. My brother and I were already accustomed to seeing deer and chipmunks. We saw them on camping trips to the Adirondack

Mountains when we were living in New York. We tied food onto strings and fed the chipmunks with Mom observing us close by. Probably a park ranger would disapprove of the activity, but we enjoyed seeing the little animals eat. Every summer, we were together as a family. The only time we went to day camp was the summers in L.A. Pop worked summers in L.A. and we only went on short family trips on the weekends and when he had vacation days. I stopped thinking about California when we were back at our tent after the walk.

We ate at a picnic table with the Petersens. They had bologna sandwiches and Mom gave us chicken sandwiches on whole wheat bread.

Mrs. Petersen asked us, "Did you hear what happened to one of the families in another section of the park?"

"What?"

"They left cereal and some snacks in their tent while they were hiking. A bear tore open the flap and ransacked their bags and ate all the food. He tore up sleeping bags, clothing, camping gear, and collapsed the tent when he ran off into the woods. The rangers said they were lucky no one was around when the bear smelled food and broke into their tent. The two rangers helped them salvage a few things and they packed up their car and left the park."

I listened to the story and clutched Mom's hand.

"I'm afraid to go to sleep tonight with so many bears around."

"Don't worry, Rozzie." By now, my eyes were big and luminous in the light filtered from the tall trees.

"All of our food is in the icebox locked in the car. The bears won't bother us tonight."

Tomorrow was our last day in Yosemite and we were going to take it easy. Mom and I were bringing our drawing pads to the lake to do some sketching. Mr. Petersen and Dad were taking the boys to do a little fishing and then, join us at the lake.

It was a good day. We went to bed early. Neither Danny nor I were looking forward to a long car ride the next day.

Chapter Nineteen

The Long Ride Home

We had a day and a half before we would reach Arizona and the Grand Canyon. Pop did most of the driving as usual and our mother drove a few hours at a stretch to relieve him so he could sleep. The radio was on and we listened to our favorite songs: Elvis Presley's hits- *Hound Dog, Don't Be Cruel,* and *Blue Suede Shoes.* We liked *Tom Dooley* by the Kingston Trio, *Rockin' Robin* by Tom Day (later a hit for the Jackson Five), *All I Have to Do is Dream* by the Everly Brothers and *The Purple People Eater* by Sheb Wooley. Our parents liked listening to *Fever* by Peggy Lee, *Catch a Falling Star* by Perry Como, and *Come Dance with Me* by Frank Sinatra—all hits of 1958. The music broke up the monotony of the long hours on the road in a car that was not air-conditioned.

Finally, the next day, we were in our campground in the Grand Canyon area. Danny and I would have liked to do the mule ride in the canyon, but Pop said it was too expensive so we walked around and took a lot of photos. We spent two days at the Grand Canyon and then Pop said we were headed for New Mexico on the famed Route 66.

Arizona was great. We all loved the Painted Desert with all of its' pastel colors, The Petrified Forest, and the Navajo Reservation, east of Flagstaff. The Native American jewelry was beautiful although costly. Pop bought Mom a silver bracelet and me, a turquoise ring that I wore for a few years until the turquoise stone cracked. It was a long distance from Arizona to New Mexico, but my brother and I loved the sights we saw along the way.

After a day and a half of driving, we were in Albuquerque, New Mexico, a historic old town established in the 1700s. After a good night's sleep, we went to the ancestral Pueblo cliff dwellings where we saw petroglyphs, the drawings painted on rocks by the ancient peoples. I think Albuquerque was one of our favorite places on the trip and an indelible memory for Danny and me. Except for Jamestown, Williamsburg, and D.C., we loved the Native American culture in New Mexico the most.

For Danny and me, this road trip was a rite of passage. We were entering a new phase of our lives—he was already a teenager and I was almost 11—between childhood and my adolescent years. Soon we would no longer share so much time together. He was going to junior high school where he would find new friends and I was going to be in sixth grade, the last year of elementary school.

The journey took us through Amarillo, Texas, Oklahoma City, Oklahoma, St. Louis, Missouri, Memphis, Tennessee, Virginia, Washington, D.C., New Jersey, and at last, New York. Pop loved explaining the history of the places we saw. In St. Louis, we went to the old court house, the site of the Dred Scott Decision. In 1847, Dred Scott and his wife, two slaves, sued for their freedom, but the court ruled against them because they were property and didn't have the right to sue. My brother and I were stunned by the idea of slavery and very saddened to learn about this unfortunate part of American history. On a better note, we visited Scott Joplin's house where he composed his ragtime classics. We liked visiting Schwab's on Beale Street in Memphis, Tennessee, the oldest store, established in 1876. Of course, of all the places we saw, Virginia was a great place to visit. We enjoyed seeing Jamestown and Williamsburg. In D.C. we went to Ford's Theater where Lincoln was assassinated, the National Zoo, the U.S. Capitol, the Jefferson and Lincoln memorials, Arlington Cemetery, and the White House. Pop was in his glory telling us a lot about U.S. history as we went to each place. I know that returning to Far Rockaway High School was the right move for Pop. He was meant to be a teacher and not a businessman.

Danny asked Pop what we were going to do when we reached our destination, "Where will we stay in New York, Pop?"

"Aunt Bea and Uncle Morris reserved a house for us in Far Rockaway where we'll spend the summer, kids."

"And then, what?" I asked.

"We're going to look for a house to buy," Mom said.

"Meanwhile Bea, Morris, Blanche and her new husband, Irv, will be waiting for us at the house in Bayswater when we arrive on Saturday," Mom explained.

We were very happy that our aunts and uncles were going to be there to greet us. Only Mom's younger sister, Blanche, came to California for a brief visit while we were living there. We hadn't seen our Aunt Bea and missed Blanche and Irv's wedding.

Chapter Twenty

Starting Over

We had been on the road for two weeks and covered three thousand miles of country. Our parents were very weary and relieved when we arrived in Far Rockaway and my mom's sisters and brothers-in-law were there to greet us on a Sunday morning. If it had been Saturday, Aunt Bea and Uncle Morris would not have been there because they didn't drive on the Sabbath. Danny and I were so excited to see them again and meet our new Uncle Irv, Aunt Blanche's new husband. We literally flew out of the car to see them.

Aunt Bea, Mom's oldest sister, kissed us first and commented," How tall you both are." Of course, Danny and I didn't get it, because our growth had been gradual during the three years we spent in California and we didn't feel any different.

The smell of the sea was in the air. Bayswater was a neighborhood just a few blocks from the beach. Aunt

Blanche suggested a stroll to the seashore after we relaxed and unpacked the car.

"Hello, Rozzie and Danny," Uncle Irv said. He smiled and hugged his new niece and nephew.

Uncle Morris always had something to give us. He hugged and kissed us and extended his hand to give each one of us a cloth patch with a saying or design on it. Uncle Morris had always been a salesman and even now, typically he was going around to small stores in Brooklyn to sell new merchandise.

"What do we do with these patches?" Danny asked.

"Your mom can sew them on your pants and jackets," he told us.

We loved our uncle. He had no children of his own, but it was obvious from his demeanor that he was fond of children. He said funny things and played games with us when he came to visit. His favorite expression was, "You can't always sometimes tell what you least expect mostly." Whenever he said it, he caught people off-guard and got a laugh from them.

We helped Mom and Pop carry our belongings into the house.

We ran to look at the bedrooms and choose which one was ours. Danny's was the larger one and I was going to have the smaller bedroom. After seeing the inside of the house, we came outside again onto the front porch. The adults were sitting on wooden rocking chairs out on the expansive veranda and we went out to be with them. We rested and talked for a while until Aunt Bea and Aunt Blanche suggested having a lunch they both prepared for all of us. They had lox, bagels, tuna fish, and salad, a dairy spread that Aunt Bea usually had on Sundays when we visited her. Uncle Irv brought cookies from Leon's Bakery, his favorite place to get cakes and cookies. He carried on the tradition years later with my children and brought them to our house when he came for lunch.

After eating, we strolled along the boardwalk with our relatives. About four o'clock, we returned to the house and they said their goodbyes and headed back to Brooklyn in Uncle Irv's reliable blue Buick.

Our parents told us that we'd be very busy that summer. We would be looking for a house and have to register in school by late August. Some days, Mom stayed with us and Pop went by himself to scout areas for homes. We had plenty of games and books from the public library. Sometimes we walked to the beach and there were other kids there to play with.

One afternoon, Pop returned and was very enthusiastic about a house he saw.

"You'll love it, Estelle. It's on a quiet street in Hewlett, not far from here. It'll only take me 20 minutes to drive to work from there."

"That sounds perfect, Saul. When are we going to see it?"

"I asked the broker to show all of us tomorrow morning."

The next day, Pop drove us to the house. It was a white clapboard Cape Cod style bungalow with a white S on the red brick chimney.

"I like the S for Schindler," Danny said to Pop.

"The owner's name is Steiner," the agent explained. "So he liked the S also."

Mom and Pop, Danny and I, explored the house, top to bottom. The first floor had two bedrooms, one bathroom, a living room with a cathedral ceiling, which Mom adored, a small dining room and kitchen. Upstairs was a tiny bedroom and a huge storage closet. Pop considered converting it to a bathroom, but never made any improvements to the house in all the years he lived there. There was an unfinished basement. It was the only room that Pop had some work done on, so we kids had a playroom. In back there was a compact yard with a huge mulberry tree that shaded the lawn. When we owned the Hewlett house, Mom had a metal device to dry clothes outdoors in the yard in warm weather when she didn't want to use the dryer in the basement. Mom loved the high ceiling in the living room. What clinched the deal was the fact that the house was in our price range. Years later when Pop died, Mom told me that she paid the down payment from her savings, a well kept secret I never knew. Pop led us to believe he bought the house. Mom felt liberated in her old age when Pop wasn't around to disagree with her.

Soon the nights were getting shorter and we were going to move into our new house by the end of August. Danny and I were already registered in the Long Island schools. We were surprised that we were no longer going to live in Queens where we had lived before. We wondered what our new neighborhood would be like.

Chapter Twenty-One
Leaving Childhood Behind

My dolls that were so precious to me I put away in my closet and only glanced at them from time to time. I was too old to play with dolls. Sixth grade girls talked a lot, learned how to dance, and rode bikes. We still played jacks and hopscotch at recess, but we were anticipating finishing elementary school and moving to the junior high school the following year.

Aunt Sarah, Uncle Harry and our grandparents were arriving the third week of June to be with us for Danny's Bar Mitzvah. Aunt Sarah and Uncle Harry were staying in a hotel and our grandparents were staying with us in our house. They were going to sleep in our parents' bedroom and our parents were setting up a cot in the living room. Mom was sleeping on the cot and Pop on the couch.

Pop warned Danny about behaving properly in school because he was tired of the phone calls complaining about

Danny's talking too much in class. Danny was quieter in class, but he still got in trouble for one ridiculous incident he and his friend were involved in. Danny and a classmate collected the metal decorations that were on top of cars' hoods. One day they saw one on a Volkswagen and took the hood ornament. What a mistake! The principal's secretary was looking out of the window and saw them do it. The ornament belonged to the principal's Volkswagen. Pop had to come to school, speak to the principal and pay for the damage. He was steaming.

"How could you take something from the principal's car?"

"I didn't think the principal of the school would drive a Volkswagen. I thought he had a Cadillac," Danny said.

"The money will come from your Bar Mitzvah gifts," he told Danny.

It was the last time Danny dared to take any more hood ornaments off cars.

The day of Danny's Bar Mitzvah arrived and we were thrilled to see our grandparents and aunt and uncle from California. Our aunts and uncles who lived in New York were beaming to share the moment with us. Uncle Morris and Aunt Bea had to sleep in our house too because they didn't drive on Saturday, the day of the Bar Mitzvah. They slept in my room and we had to get an extra cot for my uncle. I slept upstairs in the area outside of my brother's room where there was an extra bed. Imagine all of the people in my house sharing one bathroom. It was an enormous feat! Grandma Schindler was unsteady on her feet and someone always had to hold her arm when she walked around the house or had to climb the front steps to enter and exit the house. Sadly, it was the last time we saw my grandparents. When we returned to California three years later, they were gone.

Danny did well with his Haftorah and my parents were very proud of him. There was no party afterwards. Pop didn't believe in spending money on celebrations. We only had a Kiddush for our family, friends, and the temple congregation. The guests gave him checks and savings bonds that Pop put into the bank vault for him. He had to use some of the money to pay Pop back for the damage he did to his principal's car.

When the school year ended, we spent the summer at Hewlett Point Beach Club. It was a public club. You just had to be a resident of Nassau County to go there. I asked my parents if we could take Ellen from the block and they agreed. All was fine until she pulled a stunt that frightened the hell out of my parents. While we were in the pool, she feigned drowning. My mother called the lifeguard right away and was a nervous wreck. Ellen stopped flailing in the water when she saw that the lifeguard was going to pull her out of the pool. She started laughing. My parents were furious.

"Let's go home, kids," my dad said to all of us.

On the car ride home, my mom and dad sat stony-faced in silence until we deposited Ellen back at her house. They didn't say a word to her mother who was waiting on the step, but we never invited her again to the beach.

The hot summer days dwindled down and soon it meant a return to school. Danny was entering eighth grade and I was starting junior high school. It was the big time for me. I secretly hoped that I would grow taller and my shape would change from ugly duckling to graceful swan.

Chapter Twenty-Two
Jealousy,
the Green-Eyed Monster

Except for family vacations or visits to our aunts and uncles, Dan (no longer, using the kid's name, Danny) and I were on very different paths. He was semi-popular in his ninth grade class and I was struggling to make friends in eighth grade. One neighborhood girl, Barbara, was light years ahead of me in maturity and my awkward friend, Ellen, was pimply faced and not an ideal choice for a girlfriend. Besides, we clashed one day after school and were never friends again after our fight. What caused it? I find it comical now as I think about it, but it was not a laughing matter at the time. When we exited the building towards the end of the year, she asked me as she characteristically did, what grade did I have on my French test? It was one of my best subjects and I had a mark in the 90s. She had a perfect score and lorded it over me. I couldn't stand her bragging any more and said so. I don't know who punched whom first, but we were having a brawl, kicking and pulling hair, and I walked home with cuts on my face. I have a scar from that encounter that has faded over the many years since, but I can still see it in the mirror and remember when it's from. I don't know if she had any bad cuts or scratches. Luckily, she moved away at the end of eighth grade and I didn't have to face her on the block. I gave her the cold shoulder when I saw her the following school year.

High school was a scary affair for me from the first day. I remember standing in front of the new building with all of the other freshmen and being very afraid. Anything new was always tough for me. Also I was not a star pupil like my brother, Dan. I tried to copy what he did, but with limited success.

Teachers compared us since we were only one year apart and sometimes we had the same ones. But, he was charismatic and funny and I was very quiet. He was voted into the National Honor Society and I was struggling for Bs. My nemesis: math class. Fortunately, the first year of school I had a very kind math teacher, Mr. S., who promised if I worked hard, did all homework assignments and had a minimal passing test average, I would pass Algebra. Pop hired Mrs. G., to help me pass the statewide algebra exam at the end of the year and I did pull out a passing grade. The following year, I was not so fortunate in the choice of a math teacher. Mr. C. was sarcastic and very cruel. When I couldn't solve a math problem at the board, he called me "stupid" in front of the whole class. I refused to cry when he humiliated me. When I was home and in my room, I let loose and sobbed for hours until Pop came into my room and asked, "What's wrong?"

"My teacher said I was stupid because I couldn't do a problem and all of the kids laughed."

"What a jerk," my dad said and he told Mom to call the school and make an appointment for him to see the teacher.

Pop gave Mr. C. a piece of his mind and the nasty man never made fun of me again. Unfortunately, it was too late in the year for me to transfer to another teacher.

What I did like about school was being invited to sweet sixteens. One girl, Carol, was in the orchestra with me. I played second violin and she played the viola. She had talent whereas I had none, but was earning credits for being in the orchestra every year I was in school. I went to her sweet sixteen party at the Woodmere Country Club where my brother had a part-time job as a waiter. Other girls also invited me to their girls' only luncheons, but I couldn't reciprocate. I never had a party with other girls or girls and boys as some kids did. My parents invited my aunts and uncles the day of my birthday and they brought in deli sandwiches from the Woodrow, a deli that still exists in the Peninsula Shopping Center in Hewlett, New York. With every milestone, I felt I missed out on what other teens traditionally had, but I was going to be a college student some day and I was very happy about finishing high school and beginning college.

Dan was the golden child in everyone's eyes. He was able to keep up his grades, star in the school plays and work part-time to earn a little extra money. The new show was *Bye Bye Birdie* and Dan had the part of Albert Peterson. I tried out for the chorus and made it to the second tryout, but then was eliminated. I felt so deflated. When my parents and I went to see the musical, they were so proud of him and I was insanely jealous although I kept that sentiment to myself. To compound my misery, our neighbor, Barbara, sang very well and was in a lot of the school shows. She tortured me with taunts because I was quiet. The worst moments were before our teacher walked into the French class we shared. When she said mean comments to impress her friends, I tried my best to ignore her. After school, we walked home at the same time and she was with her friend and I was by myself. I can still hear her screaming at me, "You faggot." Of course those words made no sense because I wasn't gay, but in those days, it was a terrible insult. Years later, I visited the block and Barbara greeted me warmly when she saw me. I had coffee in her house and reminded her about the cruel behavior. She didn't remember anything or claimed ignorance (as one friend suggested when I told her the story) and in talking to her, I realized how different a woman she had become. She told me other kids made fun of her because she sang opera. What a shame teenagers are so unrelenting in their mean behavior I was thinking as she was complaining about her rough treatment by our peers.

The worst moment of high school was sophomore year. A group of us were waiting on line for our PSAT (Preliminary Scholastic Aptitude Results) when an announcement came over the loudspeaker system. "President Kennedy has been shot." We were stunned and crying. The principal and assistant principals were in the hall and were dismissing the school. It was a somber week—just the beginning of the overwhelmingly tragic events we experienced in the early 1960s.

There were some incredible times. 1964 was the

beginning of the British music invasion. I had a friend named Lynda who played the guitar and introduced me and our other friend, Sharon, to the Beatles. Including my older brother, who the girls had a crush on, we bought tickets to a Beatles concert at Carnegie Hall in New York. My parents agreed to let me go because Dan was with us. That day was pandemonium! The fab four sang their greatest hits to no avail. The girls were screaming so loudly you couldn't hear them. We succumbed to the hysteria and danced in the aisles. The security people couldn't stop us. There were too many people. Afterwards, we took the Long Island Railroad home and told our parents all about it. I still have the program in my possession and have shown it to my children.

Another concert my friends and I went to provided an outstanding moment for us. On a Sunday afternoon, we boarded the railroad and went to the Brooklyn Paramount Theater to see Murray the K's Rock and Roll show. He was the most popular DJ of our time and the show featured the stars of our era—Frankie Avalon and others we loved.

Three is never a good number for a friendship and I realized I was the odd person in the trio. Lynda favored Sharon over me. I was hurt when she invited her the first year of college to George Washington University to visit and I was left out. Luckily, college was a big improvement over high school and I had new friends. I quickly forgot about my high school buddies and they moved on too.

Dan graduated a year ahead of me and started Queens College. Sadly, his mental problems were plaguing him and my parents noticed changes in his behavior. I finished Hewlett High School the next year and was also going to begin Queens College. I had my heart set on going to the State University of New York at New Paltz. Pop maneuvered my life so that it wasn't going to be a reality. The school accepted me for the Summer Quarter and I had a job as a camp counselor at a camp where my dad knew the director and got me in. He said that because the college was not flexible and not allowing me to start in the fall, I should turn it down. I was devastated. Prior to applying to colleges, Pop had taken me to New York University for an IQ test. My school adviser, Mrs. W., claimed I didn't have the ability for college work because I only had an 84 overall average. But the IQ test proved I could handle college. Also, I was accepted into all three colleges I applied to. Queens College had free tuition for education majors and Pop convinced me it was the best profession for a girl. "You can work, then stay home and have a family, and after a few years, return to the workforce." It was a philosophy many girls of my era believed. Teaching, nursing, or secretarial work were all a girl could aspire to.

Strangely, I was in college with my older brother. We shared a car Pop bought for us. We drove in together and I saw him at the end of the day to go home. It did seem odd when I saw him that he was spending a lot of time in the College Memorial Center, our lounge. I was either in class or at the library doing papers or studying like the majority of the students. I didn't find out until much later that he was skipping classes and almost failing school. Pop had to beg the Dean to give him another chance.

It was advantageous to have Dan in college with me. He introduced me to some nice girls in a House Plan who accepted me into their social organization and my second year, he introduced me to the girls of Alpha Epsilon Phi Sorority. When I rushed them, they liked me and I got in. They didn't want my best friend, Marlene, another Long Island girl I met freshman year. I had to threaten to quit for them to approve her. It was a defining moment for me. I had some clout at last and felt more confident as a college girl.

Chapter Twenty-Three
Travels

The advantage of being a teacher was having the summers free. Pop didn't care about working all summer to make more money. Rather, he and Mom preferred living a frugal lifestyle so that the whole family could go on trips during the summer. When I was 14 and Dan was 16, Pop decided we should return to California to see the family. Again, we were going by car across country. What remains in my memory the most about the long ride is the young people my age we met and the kids from our own town we met in Jackson Hole, Wyoming while they were on a teen tour. Dan and I were jealous of the rich kids who were having fun and were on their own with counselors while we were with our parents. I corresponded for a while with two girls I met in small towns—one was from Paris, Idaho and I don't recall where the other was from, probably another Midwestern state. I was still writing to them when I started college. Both of them married after they finished high school and had families right away. One of them, Janlyn, had married a bigamist and had to go to court to sue for child support. She had babies with him right away. Having children was the furthest from my mind and I found that I could no longer relate to either pen pal and gradually, we stopped writing each other.

When we arrived in L.A., all dirty and sweaty from the long car ride, Cousin Francine was the first to greet Danny and me. Typical of Fran's mean behavior, she said, "You stink." I felt badly and explained that the car didn't have air-conditioning like hers and I was going to take a shower right away. Our cousin, Bob, her brother, was happy to see us and took us upstairs where Dan was going to share a room with him and I was going to be in a guest room. Uncle Harry was at work and we were going to see him when we had dinner.

It was great seeing our relatives once more. On the weekend we had plans to see Uncle Sam, Aunt Shirley, and our cousin, Bonnie, their daughter. Uncle Sam and Aunt Shirley didn't like travelling. Entertainment for them was going out to dinner and Sam didn't mind picking up the tab for everyone. One of the restaurants he liked was Fisherman's Lodge. Kids loved it because it had a fishing pond and anyone who liked to fish, could catch the trout they stocked in the pond. We felt like the poor relatives because our aunts and uncles paid for us whenever we went out. Pop was the teacher. His brothers and brother-in-law were the wealthy businessmen.

After a few days of staying in Aunt Sarah's house, we were wearing out our welcome according to Uncle Harry. While we were eating dinner one night, he commented as a supposed joke, "You know Ben Franklin believed fish and visitors smell in three days." Har, har, har, he laughed with a fat cigar wedged in his teeth. We got the hint and didn't want to stay any longer, but Pop told us in private that his relatives stayed with them numerous times and for long periods of time and Harry didn't complain, but he was less accommodating with Sarah's family. Dan and I were anticipating our departure from that household.

On one of our last days, an incident occurred that I have never forgotten. All of the aunts, uncles, and cousins were gathered in Harry and Sarah's den. I was sitting quietly listening to the conversation and Dan and Bob were outside of the house. While they were walking around the neighborhood, they spied a man stopped along the road with his car trunk open. He saw the two teenagers and began talking to them about the merchandise he was selling.

"These fine shirts are a real bargain. Usually I sell them to local stores for twice the price I 'm going to offer you. Interested, guys?"

Both Dan and Bob wanted to buy his shirts and were very happy that he was giving them such a great deal. They each bought one. The shirts were wrapped in transparent plastic. Neither Dan nor Bob took them out of the packaging to examine them.

They ran home and into the den, enthusiastic about showing everyone their bargains.

"Let's see," Aunt Sarah said and took Bob's shirt out of the wrapping. When she opened up the package, she noticed that the shirt had no sleeves.

Our aunts and uncles thought it was funny and all of us were laughing. But, Uncle Harry was not even smiling.

He screamed at his son, "Schmuck. How can you throw money away like that?"

Bob's face reddened and he ran to his room so that he wouldn't cry in front of the family. His sister was especially cruel and he didn't want to hear her taunts.

Dan's shirt had sleeves, but it was made of a very shoddy material. He was embarrassed, but our parents didn't make any disparaging remarks. Pop told him it was a good lesson he and Bob learned. "Next time, you'll look more carefully at something you're buying."

And he did when we were home.

I was glad we went to California that summer. It was going to be a long time before I was going to visit the family again. I didn't go back until I was a single girl in my 20's and flew there with a girlfriend who wanted to see L.A.

Most of our trips were family vacations except for the tour of Europe my parents went on without Dan and me. It must have been the summer when I finished the sixth grade and Dan ended his first year of junior high school. Aunt Bea and Uncle Morris stayed in our house while Mom and Pop were on their two-week excursion. We loved having our aunt and uncle take care of us because they played a lot of games and didn't enforce a bedtime because it was the summer and they didn't mind if we slept late the next day. We played a lot of Scrabble, a game I still love. They called it, "Scrabble Night with the Berkowitz's," when we played with them. I think they let Dan and me win so we would want to play more games. If we lost, we wouldn't want to play Scrabble. Aunt Bea nudged Uncle Morris and made sure we won.

When our parents came home, of course we were happy. They brought us some gifts and presents for Aunt

Bea and Uncle Morris. We were sorry that we didn't have our aunt and uncle as babysitters again.

Chapter Twenty-Four
Troubled Times

The world was a turbulent place in the 1960s. Black people and women were fighting for their civil rights and a war was raging in Viet Nam. The college campuses reflected the concerns of the nation. Dan and I were upset about the disruptions taking place. Mom and Pop were against the war and going on peace marches. There was a lot of hostility towards them. The hawks and doves were at odds. At Pop's school, the history teachers were divided. More of them supported the war and didn't agree with Pop. At Queens College, the student leaders organized protests. The issues were the war, civil rights, and students' rights. Students didn't want required subjects, but the right to choose their studies. Students for a Democratic Society or S.D.S. led the opposition. A lot of the students were using drugs openly in the College Memorial Center. When I walked in there, the smell of pot was everywhere. I suspected that my brother, Dan, was experimenting with drugs, but didn't want to say anything to our parents. Dan looked like the radicals. He sported a scruffy beard, had long, shaggy hair and smoked a pipe like our professors. He had a corduroy jacket with suede patches and wore jeans all the time. I suspected drug use too. Dan was still handsome and a charmer, but he was different. I surmised he was having a lot of difficulties and I didn't want to add to them.

His first year of college, he drove the car into the garage and left the motor running. If Pop hadn't found him, he would have been asphyxiated by the carbon monoxide. My parents brought him to a psychiatrist, the husband of one of my mom's private sculpture students. Dan was diagnosed with bipolar disorder. Aunt Bea thought that the Mumps he had the year before when he was a camp counselor in upstate New York caused Dan's mental illness. Who knows the cause? The consequences of the illness were tragic for Dan, my parents, and me.

There were moments when Dan enjoyed life. He met a girl his senior year. Judy was a freshman and completely in love with my brother. She was four years his junior, very thin, and had her nose done, but was attractive with her long straight dark hair and preppy clothing. I liked her a lot and was glad that my brother was happy for a change.

In 1967, I was in my second year at Queens College and struggling to achieve good grades. I still was having difficulty with math and science. The only subjects I was doing well in were Spanish, art history, and poetry. I spent hours in the library on campus and at home and I spent a lot of time on papers and studying for exams. I was concentrating a lot on myself, my studies, and when I had time, my social life. I wondered why Dan was seldom in the library and seemed to be in the CMC a lot.

Dan's illness was terrible, but the great shock to fracture our family life was the news that Uncle Lou, Pop's youngest brother, shot his wife to death on the evening of April 9, 1967. Uncle Sam called Pop the next day to recount the horrific story.

Years later I heard this account about that night: Lou's wife was on the phone with her close friend and joking about being in love with another man. She had filed for a divorce weeks earlier. The law had this husband and wife living together even though Lou was insanely jealous. The Swedish maid upstairs with their infant daughter was startled by a loud noise from the kitchen. Lou shot his wife June seven times. Five bullets entered her body. He walked out of the kitchen, went into the garage, took a bicycle, and rode away. He called his older brother, Sam, and his attorney who advised surrendering at the police station in Bel Air. Meanwhile, the maid went downstairs to investigate. Her mortally wounded employer told her to seek help at the fire station on the corner. June staggered outside and died in the garden. Lou was convicted of second-degree murder, but won two appeals because of bad jury instruction. He was released on probation after pleading guilty to involuntary manslaughter. He had served two years in federal prison. For the two years he was away, Lou's wife's family had custody of their baby grandchild. After his release from prison, Lou regained custody of his daughter much to the dismay of the grieving grandparents. They hated the Schindlers for all of the years they lived.

My cousin, Francine, a hairdresser, introduced Lou to one of her clients; a very attractive divorcee and former model named Laura. He married her after knowing her a short time and designated this glamour girl as his baby Kim's stepmother. Lou and Laura were married for seven years from 1971 until 1978. Incredibly, like an episode of a soap opera, his third wife shot him while he was sleeping. She claimed that Lou had abused her for years and she was afraid of him. The autopsy proved that she was slowly poisoning her husband. The blonde bombshell, although jail made her less attractive, was convicted of second-degree murder. However, she won an appeal on a technicality just as Lou had twelve years before. Her defense attorney won the appeal on the grounds that the prosecutor violated her Miranda rights during a jailhouse interview. She was in jail less than two years. It was time served while awaiting her trial.

Lou's sister and brothers were distraught by the verdict. Only Aunt Shirley said to "move on." Ironically Aunt Shirley's words didn't ring true. One day, four or five years after the verdict, my Aunt Sara saw Lou's ex-wife at a swap meet. She recognized Laura, no longer the wealthy suburban woman. Laura was older and dressed in plain jeans and tee shirt. Aunt Sara screamed at the top of her lungs, "Murderer, murderer," when she saw her and people stared and wondered what was going on. Her best friend grabbed her arm and pulled her away from the booth where Laura was selling her flea market wares.

Chapter Twenty-Five
Independence

I didn't have a co-ed college dorm experience. I was attending a commuter city school, living at home and sharing a car with my older brother who had it more than I did. He had a girlfriend and used the car on weekends to take her out. Sometimes I had the car when I went to my friend Marlene's house in Plainview, a 40-minute drive across Long Island. I had the habit of keeping an overnight bag in my car so I could sleep at friends' houses if I was out very late at night and didn't want to come home and disturb my parents.

One night, while sitting on the floor of her bedroom, we talked about our summer plans. I was going on a study program abroad to Spain and Marlene, a history major, was going on a school program to Corsica, Italy. I was so excited. I had never been away from home before. Some of my sorority sisters were going on the trip also and I felt more secure because at least I knew a few people on the trip.

During the school year, I wanted to earn a little spending money. I was working as a tutor for the S.E.E.K program, a special project that paved the way for minority students to attend college free of charge. They received weekly stipends for school and the Spanish majors among them were going gratis on the summer progam to Spain. I was enthusiastic about tutoring, but was shocked when it became clear that my students had no intentions of showing up for the tutoring sessions. Their attendance was not mandatory and they were getting their stipends regardless if they had tutoring or not. I eventually quit the S.E.E.K Program and had a new job as a sales girl at Mays Department Store. I worked in the Boutique Department and helped girls buy expensive items like wedding gowns. It was hard work, but I loved having the extra cash in my pocket.

It was increasingly difficult to live at home because I had so little privacy. The phone extensions were either in the living room where Mom and Pop sat on the couch or in their bedroom. They could hear my phone conversations and sometimes, interrupted them. God! I could not wait until I was able to afford my own place.

Finally, it was July and I was at the airport waiting with the other students for the flight to Europe. I was so nervous.

I had a bad case of diarrhea before boarding the plane. I think it was the Shrimp Scampi I ate at the Carolina diner. I have never eaten that dish again. At the airport, my black suitcase was enormous and I struggled to lug it to the desk where it was put on the conveyor belt. It was stuffed with dresses from Loehmann's. In those days, the designers cut out the labels of dresses that were unsold and Loehmann's bought them and sold them to savvy shoppers for much cheaper prices. I wanted to be sure I was stylish and had enough to wear for the eight weeks in Spain.

First destination: Paris, France. Already, I made friends with three girls I didn't know at Queens College—Bette, Ronnie, and Chris. We stayed together the three days we were in France. I kind of forgot about my sorority sisters.

My new friends and I met an American family at our hotel. They lived in Maspeth, Queens and it was their first trip abroad. When we walked around the Red Light District at night, they were ahead of us on the block. Prostitutes were everywhere. My friend, Bette, was wearing a provocative miniskirt and a Frenchman propositioned her. She turned to our American dad and his family and said, "Papa." The Frenchman realized his error and quickly ran.

The travel was exhausting and both Bette and I

developed health problems. She had a stomach virus and the hotel doctor prescribed suppositories. We had to buy French yoghurt in a small grocery store for her—doctor's orders. I was taking antibiotics for an infection in my right arm. Before going on the trip, I was bitten by a spider in my backyard. Our doctor prescribed medicine that I was taking, but the infection was getting worse. It looked like I had a golf ball inside my forearm. My friends, Ronnie, Bette, and Chris insisted on taking me to the American Hospital in Paris. Bette was the most fluent in French and explained what was wrong. The doctor suggested waiting two more days until we were in Spain and could find a doctor there.

We had some time in Madrid before our summer courses were starting. My three friends accompanied me to the University of Madrid hospital. I was running a fever. The doctor said he would operate on the arm and remove the infection. I didn't want to go home so I agreed to the surgery. I had dressings on my arm for many weeks and couldn't write. My professor gave me the option of dictating answers orally to his exams on Don Quixote and the grammar lessons for the second course. I didn't write to my parents and they became worried and called the university. I confessed what happened and surprisingly, they didn't insist that I return home. Fantastic!

On weekends, my friends and I travelled to other towns by train. We bought tickets for third class passage to Granada one weekend. It was so crowded that we had to toss our luggage through the windows. We couldn't buy food. Fortunately we were sitting next to a young man and his sister and they offered us some of their chicken and bread. We drank their wine too from big skins they carried. When Bette and I got up to find the bathroom, a group of leering Portuguese men pinched her vagina. We screamed at the laughing fools and hit them with our bags as we climbed over passengers' possessions to reach the bathroom. It was disgusting, but we were desperate to relieve ourselves.

Thirteen harrowing hours by cattle-car train ride later, we were in Granada. There were no vacancies in hotels because it was the height of the vacation season for Europeans, but the tourist information center representative told us we could stay in someone's home. We took the address and rang the bell of a modest house in the city. A toothless, hunchbacked old lady answered the door and showed us our room. The bathroom was down the hall. We were scared in that lodging and laughed to ourselves that the woman was a "bruja." (witch)

My friends and I had many great adventures like the one I mentioned in Granada. We met Spanish boys, went out with them in groups (not safe to be unchaperoned), and socialized with Americans we met, mostly young fresh-faced boys who were in the armed services. We loved touring the capital city every chance we had after classes. We strolled through El Parque del Buen Retiro that was like Central Park in New York, went to the zoo, the Prado art museum, and the many shops downtown. We especially liked the department store, El Corte Ingles, and bought some clothing and shoes there. Chris taught me to be frugal with my money and stretch out what I had to last the whole summer. I followed her advice when we were on our final two-week tour of the northern cities and bought a small table with a music box made of inlaid wood, some material to make a skirt, and gifts for my parents and brother. Sadly, several years later, I smashed that delicate table in a rage when I had a spat with my husband over some trivial matter that I cannot even remember now. Foolhardy.

Chris and I spoke about going back to Spain so we could learn the language. Both of us were going to be Spanish teachers when we graduated. Bette was a French major and undecided about what she wanted to do. Ronnie was studying Psychology. The only girl I remained friends with was Chris and we did return to Europe after college and went to Mexico together too.

Marlene told me all about her experiences in Corsica. She hitchhiked all around the island and to other places in Europe. Marlene was in love with her history professor who went along on that student trip as a chaperone, a man old enough to be her father. I questioned how wise it was to be having an affair with an older man. She said it was the '60s and the world was changing for women. I didn't know how fast things were evolving. The majority of the girls in our classes at Queens College were engaged and getting married as young as their mothers did. Most were going to be teachers and help support their husbands who were going to law school or medical school.

1967 was a mild year compared to 1968, a year that I wouldn't forget.

Chapter Twenty-Six
Rebellion

1968 was a turbulent time. The campus was heating up. A lot of the students were protesting the war and the rules the college imposed on them. Some of the student leaders took over buildings. The administration negotiated with them in order to quell the disruption.

Small changes were gradually taking place. The girls no longer had to wear skirts. We were permitted to wear slacks during the winter months when it was so cold outside. It was a welcome new policy, but sadly I think the end of a dress code ushered in a new style that was sloppy. When students and instructors began wearing jeans, people looked unkempt. I never liked the jeans girls wore. Since the boys had long hair as well as the girls, sometimes you couldn't tell if you were seeing a boy or girl unless he had a mustache or beard.

I wanted to earn some college credits during the summer so I could graduate on time. One of the classes I had taken sunk my grade point average. Stupidly, I registered for physics the first semester and didn't realize how difficult a subject it was for me. I was a poor math student and could not navigate through the rigors of physics. By mid-semester, I was failing. I asked my professor if I could drop the class. I had passed the deadline for dropping out. He analyzed my test scores and told me what grade I needed on the Final Exam to pass his course. The last exam was a surreal experience. Even though I studied, I stared at the questions and my mind was a blank. I couldn't even recognize the names of the great men in physics—the easy questions. I thought I was going to faint and asked the proctor to let me go to the ladies' room and get some water. I was one of the last people to leave the exam room, but I knew I failed miserably. Sure enough, when the grades came in the mail, I had a big four-credit F in the class. My G.P.A. was in the toilet. I was so upset. Even though I had good grades in my other classes, my overall average stank. I had to take geology the following semester, a very boring science and had longer course hours to compensate for the failure in physics. But, at least I was able to achieve a B.

My social life was going pretty well. I was meeting some guys at Frat parties and meeting some of them in my classes too. One of the guys I met in Spanish class was a lively young redhead named Jerry. My brother nicknamed him, "Cuff-link," because he liked to wear shirts with French cuffs and cufflinks. On one of our dates, he took me ice-skating one frigid afternoon in Grant Park near where I lived. He had played a lot of ice hockey and was a great skater. He jumped over barrels and did a lot of speedy maneuvers. I was not much of a skater and was glad to hold his arm as we skated. He was a fun person and we stayed together during the duration of our Spanish class. He was a terrible language student and was glad I could help him with our assignments. But, it wasn't kismet and we both mutually broke off the relationship. Shortly afterwards, I met Ricky. He was very good-looking with his dark hair and blue eyes. He played the guitar and sang and in between classes, we sat outside in the sun and he strummed his guitar and sang folk songs that were popular that year. We went out a lot on Friday nights. I asked my friend, Marlene, what she thought about him not asking me out on a Saturday night and then I found out from another student that Ricky had a girlfriend. She pointed the girl out to me when we were in the student lounge. That was the end of my interest in Ricky. I told him that I didn't want to be second fiddle and he was not breaking up with his girlfriend, so we parted company. It was a learning curve for me.

I was looking forward to the summer. Since, I needed to study in the summer so I could graduate on time next year, I signed up for an intensive Portuguese course at the University of Wisconsin in Madison. I was going alone to a place far from home. It was terrifying for a girl who was so sheltered by her parents.

I went to my dorm in Elizabeth Waters Hall and entered the very empty room. My roommate wrote me a note and left it on the bed that was mine. Her name was Torchy and she was from Colorado Springs, Colorado. She was away for the weekend, but was coming back in time for orientation. I was completely on my own that Saturday and Sunday. I ate in the cafeteria and watched T.V. in the dorm lounge with a few other students who were there ahead of time like me. I went back to my room each night and cried on my pillow because I felt so lonely. But, I thought it'd be all right when the classes began.

Torchy introduced herself and she was a perky, friendly person—very petite with a short reddish pixie-cut hairdo. I had my Vidal Sassoon haircut that summer. I spent 65 dollars at an upscale New York salon—a lot of money in 1968 for a broke college student, but I wanted to look sophisticated. My chestnut brown hair was sculpted into a cap with points of hair on both sides of my face and a point in the back of my skull. I thought it was very sophisticated and my roommate complimented it. She was 25 and taking college classes to improve her resume and become qualified for a better job. I told her I was 20 and still an undergraduate at a college in New York. She had never been to New York, but said she wanted to go there some day.

Before classes began, I met a cute guy who was a football player and he was in summer school to repeat a class he had failed during the year. We hung out for a while and then I didn't see him any more once my course began. It was an intensive Portuguese class—eight credits, four hours a day for eight weeks. The class was divided into different topics: grammar, literature, writing, and conversation. There was more than one instructor. One was a professor and the other, a young instructor. The students were a diverse group. Some of them were missionaries and needed to know Portuguese for their work in Brazil. Some of the people were language majors like me and wanted to study another language.

I loved the class and was very happy I came to the University of Wisconsin. It was a beautiful school and Madison was a very lovely small city.

One day after class, one of the students approached and started talking to me. He complimented me on one of my cute outfits. It was a short floral dress with a matching little cloth bag (from Loehmann's, of course). I was flattered and flirted with him. He asked me to meet him at the rathskeller later on in the afternoon and go over our assignment. Hmm, I was thinking—this is what happened with Jerry at Queens College. He wanted me to help him with Spanish and then we went out.

I'll call him C. He was from Georgia, 25, and studying anthropology at the University of Illinois, Carbondale. I had no idea where his school was. But, I liked him right away. He also was a former football player, about five ten, and had wavy dirty-blonde hair and very big blue eyes. We went out a lot that summer and he was a perfect gentleman.

I met a group of South American students who were at the school to learn English. I stayed with them at lunchtime to practice Spanish and they asked me to speak English with them so they could learn more English. I particularly bonded with one girl named Consuelo from Lima, Peru. She too was five years older that I and was studying English for her work in an American perfume company based in Lima. She missed her fiancé in Lima and I did my best to cheer her up. She told me that she was taking the advanced English class in the fall and didn't have anywhere to go when the summer session ended. I called my parents and asked them to let me invite Consuelo to stay with us for this interim period. My parents were surprised, but said yes. When I told Consuelo the news, she was ecstatic.

The Portuguese class was going very well. One of my teachers, whom we called David, asked a few students including me to recite poetry for a presentation held for other professors in the language department. It was a lot of fun. Our final project was an oral presentation that the whole class was doing as part of our grade. One of the students wrote a play and gave out parts to all of us. She was a Spanish instructor at Queens College and was studying Portuguese as a second language. Our teachers loved the play and all of us benefitted by learning a lot of Brazilian Portuguese.

I was very sad to leave C. He promised to write and call and come to New York after his first semester of college ended this coming year.

Consuelo bought a plane ticket for New York and we flew home together. We only spoke Spanish on the flight.

It was really intense and I was getting a headache from concentrating so much, but I was glad to be her friend. I hoped to go to Peru and visit her some day.

Chapter Twenty-Seven
Senior Year of College

After the Portuguese course ended in August, Consuelo and I returned home to my house in Hewlett. My mother set up a cot in my bedroom for Consuelo. My parents and brother liked my friend, but had difficulty communicating with her since her English was so limited. Since they didn't speak Spanish, her English had to improve. Dan asked her if she'd like to see Manhattan one afternoon and Consuelo was excited about going to the city with us on the Long Island Railroad and the subway. We explained that first we were coming into Penn Station and then we were going to take the subway to Greenwich Village. The train was crowded.

"There's the train. Get on fast, girls." I rushed onto the subway, but the doors closed and Consuelo didn't get on with me.

"Oh no. What do we do?" I asked my brother.

"Maybe she'll call our parents. There are phone booths all around the city."

"Let's get off at the next stop and maybe she'll take the subway here."

We waited a long time and didn't see her. We called home and Mom said she didn't call. We decided to go home.

Consuelo was in the house before us. "Que paso?" "What happened?" I asked her in Spanish.

She remembered that she had to take the Long Island Railroad to Hewlett. She thought we would have taken the train back to Penn Station and found her, but when she didn't see us there, she took the train by herself and walked back to the house.

Dan and I hugged and kissed her and promised not to lose her again.

During the two weeks she was with us, I took her to the beach, the mall, and to my friend Marlene's house. She had to speak English with Marlene and her mother who was home while we were there.

Pop made it clear to Consuelo that her visit was going to be two weeks only because we were going on a family trip before college started after Labor Day. She made plane reservations for her return to the University of Wisconsin. I promised to continue writing to her. We kept up our correspondence for a few years and some time after I finished college and was working as a teacher, she came into New York on a business trip. I was in school, but my parents were at home when she called and they went to Kennedy Airport to see her. She gave them gifts and had a Peruvian poncho for me that I still have in the trunk in the spare bedroom of my house in Florida.

My friend C. from Portuguese class called after class ended and I was back in NY and he was in his college in Illinois. He was going to visit me during the Christmas holiday. He drove his Volkswagen bus to Long Island. He was going to spend a long weekend with my family and me.

It was a magical time in the city. The store windows on Fifth Avenue were decorated for the holiday and there was snow on the ground. We took the train into the city and rode on a bus along Fifth Avenue. C. bought tickets for the new musical, *Hair*. We sat up in the nosebleed section in the balcony. It was hard to see. Still, the show was great and shocking with the nude scene at the end.

My house was so tiny. There was no extra guest room. C. had to sleep on the couch in the living room. I wondered what he thought of my modest home. It was awkward too that Pop asked him so many questions.

When he went back to Illinois, I cried. I wondered when we would see each other again.

I sat on the floor of Marlene's room and we talked about how our lives were changing. I told her how much I cared for C. A long-distance romance was going to be a challenge, she told me. After school ended, she was going to graduate school in California. She wanted to be a journalist. I was going to be a Spanish teacher and hoped to land a good job at a Long Island high school.

The only class that Marlene and I were taking together senior year was camping—her idea. It was Pass/Fail and according to Marlene, mostly guys took the course and it would be a fun way to meet them. Fortunately, she had ended the affair with her history professor and was again interested in students her own age.

I had a crush on one of the guys in our class. His name was Carl and I was hoping he would ask me out, but I didn't know if he had a girlfriend. He offered to drive Marlene and me to the camping trip in Bear Mountain. He and his friend were smoking pot out the car windows and Marlene and I were nervous about police stopping the car. However, we managed to arrive at the campsite without incident. Marlene had been to summer camps, so she set up her tent easily. I asked Carl if he would help me and he set my pup tent up for me. Our camping teacher, Mr. W., came along with his clipboard and grading sheet and checked off the completed tents. It was freezing overnight and there was snow on the ground when we woke up. One student, a masculine-looking girl, was backing out of a tent and Mr. W. thought it was a boy with long hair. He was flustered when the kid said her name was Susan. None of us laughed because we didn't want to hurt her feelings. She was a good sport about it anyway. We picked up our packs after breakfast and went on a five-mile hike in the mountains. It was pretty rigorous.

I decided I didn't want to go on the second camping trip and made an excuse that I was sick. The class was Pass/Fail and I did pass despite not waking up at four in the morning to meet the class on a Long Island beach.

Graduation day was approaching. Dan stayed an extra year to make up credits and was graduating the same year I was. I didn't want to attend our graduation, but our parents insisted on seeing us both graduate. In 1969, campuses were rife with protest even on graduation day. There was graduation and counter-graduation. A group stood up during commencement and left. They held their protest graduation in another location from where we were.

I didn't expect gifts. For high school graduation, I wanted a charm bracelet and Mom convinced Pop to buy me one. I wore it for a lot of years and added more charms to it when I could afford to buy them.

Chapter Twenty-Eight
Working Girl

I went on a lot of interviews hoping to have a teaching position in a Long Island school. I wasn't hired anywhere. I decided to apply for a city high school, but there were more teachers than openings. It was difficult to find an opening in a good high school, but I needed a job and was willing to accept one in Brooklyn or Queens. The person in charge of hiring at the Board of Education wanted to place me in a horrible school. His secretary, a nice Jewish lady from Queens advised me to turn down the first school that was terrible and wait for the next position. I listened to her advice and was placed in Richmond Hill High School in Queens. It wasn't a very good school, but not so bad either and I was eager to begin teaching Spanish.

Coincidentally, Dan's mother-in-law was an art teacher at Richmond Hill and was very helpful my first days at the school. Dan and his college girlfriend had gotten married the summer of 1969. She was still a college student in her last year and Dan became an elementary school teacher. His first assignment was in Chinatown. He and his wife had an apartment in Briarwood, Queens, a residential area close to Forest Hills. We were all very busy and I rarely saw Dan and his wife, Judy.

I liked teaching Spanish and was trying very hard to present lessons that the students enjoyed. The only glitch was my supervisor. She was a single, middle-aged woman who relished being the boss. Ruth was in my classroom frequently to observe her new teacher. That was okay, but she undermined me in front of my students with constant criticism. I was hoping she would leave me alone once I had more experience and was in the school for a few years.

How naïve I was. School budgets were always a problem. Money was tight and teachers were expendable. A lot of teachers were going to be excessed from the school at the end of the first semester. Last hired were the first fired, so I was in the danger zone since I was a new teacher. I wasn't fired. I was excessed, which meant I was going to be placed in another high school. In January, I was assigned to John Adams High School in another part of Queens. This time, I realized that the position wasn't permanent. I would have to wait a while until I had a more stable placement.

At John Adams, I had to teach art and Spanish because there weren't enough Spanish classes for everyone in my department. I was assigned to the Annex building that housed the ninth grade students. I was happy there. The only negative experience was the one I am going to relate. One day I wore a pair of dark brown suede culottes to school. I thought it was a great outfit—a pretty brown tweed top with the suede culottes and boots. The principal of the Annex didn't agree with my fashion statement. He called me over, "Miss Schindler, your skirt is too short. Your attire is inappropriate. Please go home and change and I'll get another teacher to cover your program until you return."

Whoa, I thought. How old-fashioned. I didn't want to be insubordinate and so, I drove home, changed outfits, and was back for my last class of the day. What a waste of time I thought, but I know better from now on to dress more conservatively.

Again, even though I was well liked in the school, I was excessed at the end of the year. This time, I didn't cry when I was given a pink slip and reassigned to Lafayette High School in Brooklyn. The travel was more arduous from Hewlett, but the school was okay.

One of the secretaries had a son who was in my Spanish class. Luckily, he was a decent student and a nice kid. So, there never was an issue. When I was again excessed at the end of the year, she regretted that I wouldn't be her son's teacher.

At my new school, my chairman gave me good write-ups after observing me and I was learning a lot and becoming a good teacher. However, he had one big negative opinion of me. When I came back from Puerto Rico after Christmas vacation, I wore a wig to school to cover up my unkempt hair. I was too tired to wash it so I put on a gypsy wig that was a golden color- not at all like my natural chestnut brown hue. He called me aside and was very insulting. "What is that thing on your head?" I was offended and told him so. He insisted that I go home. It was already after lunch and I only had two classes to go. I told him that I lived far away and would not be able to come back on time. "Go," he said. "We'll talk tomorrow."

That incident didn't affect my reputation in the Foreign Language Department and yet, I wasn't appointed to Lafayette High School. For September, I received an appointment in the mail for New Utrecht High School, another school in Brooklyn not far from this one.

I remained at New Utrecht for twenty-three years and except for the three years I was excessed to Sarah J. Hale in downtown Brooklyn, most of my career was spent there.

Chapter Twenty-Nine
The Single Life

Some aspects of my life remained steady, but there were disruptions to my happiness. I was 22 and thought I was unique among my peers. Many of the college grads I knew were married and planning their futures with husbands. I had to find girls like me to befriend who were single and wanted to socialize. My friend, Chris, one of the girls who went with me on the summer study program in Spain, had similar goals—she wanted to travel, learn Spanish, and meet someone to marry. We planned a return to Spain in the summer when we had a vacation.

Meanwhile, my beloved Aunt Bea was very ill. She had breast cancer and the disease was spreading to her brain. My mother told me years later that Aunt Bea, who nurtured everyone in her family, neglected herself. She ignored the tumor in her breast and let the cancer progress to the worst stage before going to the doctor. I don't know if early intervention in those years would have saved her life, but neglecting the disease, accelerated her demise. Our family was devastated when she passed away. Uncle Morris, her husband, was lost without Aunt Bea. His brother-in-law, Irv, and sister-in-law, Blanche, helped him with life's daily chores and a few years later, Blanche introduced him to Tillie, a single, religious woman, who had never married and was a good match for Morris. Their marriage was solid, but Tillie was no Aunt Bea. She was set in her ways and resented Morris' naps on their couch and a few more ingrained habits that she didn't like. Still, the marriage functioned and we liked her. We went to visit Tillie and Morris and enjoyed her home-baked cookies and pleasant demeanor. We did notice the light went out in Uncle Morris's eyes. He stopped telling his silly jokes and was more serious and religious.

My aunt's death dampened my spirit for a while. Yet, I continued to go forward. Chris and I hung out on the weekend. I went to the Irish bars with her, but felt like a fish out of water. She flirted expertly and dated some of the handsome guys we met. I didn't. On the weekends we went to Jones Beach. Sometimes she had to bring her little brother, John, along with us because her parents ran Baker's Variety Store in Hewlett on Saturdays.

Four girls, two of Chris's friends and us, were meeting in Europe and traveling together. Chris, Claudine, and Jean went to France first and I was meeting them there at Claudine's aunt and uncle's home in Dourdan, a small town an hour outside of Paris. It was exciting for me to use my French to get myself on a train bound for the countryside and communicate in that language with French people in the small town. We waited about a week for a car that Michel, Claudine's cousin, a mechanic, was finding for us to purchase for our journeys through France, Portugal, and Spain. The plan was to resell the MG1100 at the end of the summer before going home. While we were in Dourdan, we bonded with the young inhabitants like Daniel, a dashing young man, who drove us to Paris to sightsee and took us all around his town. Four American girls who appreciated his charms surrounded him.

Finally, Michel checked out the car and approved it mechanically. We said goodbye to Claudine's family and began our trip. Jean decided not to go with us because she had relatives in Germany she was going to visit. Three of us were going to drive together through France, Spain, Portugal, and Italy. I was the only one who didn't drive a stick shift and Chris resented me sitting in the back of the car while she did a lot of the driving. I tried to soothe the ruffled feathers by paying for the gas and she was better when I did.

Our trip was punctuated by adventures. We picked up a British hitchhiker in Spain.

"Is this a good idea?" I asked the girls.

"We're all tall, robust girls and he's a thin, slightly-built guy our age. I think it's all right," said Chris and I took her word for it.

He helped with some of the driving until we dropped him off somewhere in Portugal.

Our next encounter was with Chet, a wealthy California guy, who was driving an expensive sports car. We ate lunch together and followed his car to our next destination.

Along the route in Italy, we met two good-looking California motorcycle riders. One of them had a terrible injury on his leg from falling off his bike. We helped him clean out the wound and advised him to go to a hospital. Before they left, they gave us rides in the Alps on their bikes. We loved the experience and were sad to see them go.

A funny incident occurred in Italy. The clutch on our car malfunctioned and in order to get the car started, we had to push it downhill to pop the clutch and start it. The Italians leered at three big American girls pushing the car and jumping in once it was going. We didn't know much Italian and yet we had to explain what was wrong with the car when we finally found a garage and a mechanic. Chris had studied a little Italian and she was our interpreter. Words and gestures got the point across and we had our car back in good running condition.

Chris and I spent a lot of time in Spain. Claudine opted to go home. We loved every minute of our trip and even thought of staying in Spain for a year to teach English at Berlitz. A man we met at Montjuich (an amusement park atop a mountain) who worked at a radio station in Barcelona was going to help us get an apartment. His name was Alfonso Monso, a portly middle-aged man who was five feet tall and five feet wide. We met his wife and child when we were invited to his home. We were grateful for his help and friendship.

It was strange what happened next. Chris went back to the states to be with her boyfriend, Warren. She promised me that if she weren't serious about him, she would return right away to share an apartment with me and we would look for jobs.

Mr. Monso did help with apartment hunting, but the hovel he said I could afford was depressing. It was tiny, shabby, and just had a hot plate—no kitchen. I tired of waiting for Chris' decision and was anxious to go home. I couldn't cope with the loneliness of being a foreigner in a difficult culture for a woman. I wanted to see Paris again, one of my favorite cities in Europe. I had to get a ticket for home after my last hurrah in The City of Lights.

I stayed in a cheap pension on the left bank. I was lonely. I caught the eye of a Canadian girl while I was sitting at a café having lunch. We began talking and swapping stories about our adventures in Italy and France. She was glad to have female company and to be able to talk freely. In Rome, she had a horrific experience with a young man she thought was safe to go out with. He nearly raped her. I had a similar bad experience the night before I met this girl. Someone tapped on my hotel room door. When I foolishly opened it, a swarthy young man threw me on the bed and I feared he intended to rape me. He was very tiny and I overpowered him weight-wise. I yelled at the top of my lungs, struck him with my fists, and was so angry at the intrusion that I ran down the stairs after him. He was scared off. I went to the desk and asked the clerk to call a gendarme. The jerk laughed at my story. Shaking, I went back to my room, grabbed a jacket and determined to avoid the hotel; I walked to the corner and bought a movie ticket for *MASH*, a new American film that I watched multiple times. I was afraid to stay at that miserable pension. We commiserated as the Canadian girl listened to my story and then parted company before nightfall. I think we both were apprehensive of staying outside in the dark by ourselves. She was leaving for home the next day and so was I. I had a ticket on Icelandic Airlines (the so-called hippy airline); it was very cheap leaving from nearby Luxembourg. I was taking a bus to the small neighboring country of Luxembourg for the flight. It made an unexpected stop in the capital of Iceland because there was a crazy man onboard who was threatening the passengers. He was taken into custody when we landed. I had a few hours to shop and bought wool gloves, a sweater, and a few other trinkets for my family that I gave them when I arrived at JFK.

Whew! It was good to be back in the USA!

Chapter Thirty

Teaching and More Travel

Teaching, socializing, and planning more travel in the summer was all- involving. I concentrated on myself and didn't do much at home. Mom still was the chief cook and bottle washer. I cleaned my room—maybe. Living at home was easy, but I didn't like the lack of privacy. The house was so small that when my parents heard me making plans, they sometimes interrupted my conversations with their comments. I did not feel like an adult.

Chris and I were going to travel to Mexico this summer. To save money we took buses around the country. We went to Texas and from the border, we chose Flecha Roja to go into Mexico. It was quite an experience. The bus driver's radio was playing the Beatles and Mexicans had cages with chickens on their laps, when a boy and girl got on. He was dressed as Jesus with muslin gown and crown of thorns on his head and she looked like a young disciple of his. Their destination was a town with a religious festival. The bus had a name, Lupita, and sported colorful pompoms hanging from the top of the inside window. We chatted with the passengers near us and they were amazed that we were by ourselves on the trip. Girls in Mexico did not travel alone.

Mexico City was fun, but because we were two girls unaccompanied by men, the male population thought we were fair game and verbally assaulted us and occasionally someone touched us inappropriately in a crowded market or city area. They called us "fresas" or strawberries because we were "gringas". Once an old man pinched my butt while we were buying souvenirs in the marketplace. I turned around to slap him and saw that he had trouble walking with his cane. I said to my friend, "Let him enjoy himself. His days on earth are measured." She laughed. We saw everything in the capital: art museums, parks, and the zoo. At the zoo, we heard kids saying, "Foca, foca." It meant "seal." The word was even funnier in French, "foque." We wrote all new vocabulary in our notebooks. We journeyed outside of the city to Tenochtitlan to see the pyramids of the sun and moon. Travel by bus was exhausting and we were just having two meals a day—Chris's idea of budgeting our money to maximize our time in Mexico. I was losing weight and even squeezed myself into the clothes she lent me. We shared outfits because we didn't bring a lot of them and we got tired of wearing the same thing over and over.

We rode all the way down to Acapulco by bus and looked for lodging near the beach, where we found an inexpensive hotel. At the beach one day, we spied from afar two young Mexicans; one was our height and was carrying a parrot on his shoulder. The other, El Feo (the ugly one), was very tall and had an Aztec nose and profile. They were very friendly, so we felt comfortable with them immediately. I had a stomachache and was going to buy Alka Seltzer somewhere. El Feo suggested going to his house and he would make me some Manzanilla tea. I wondered if it was a good idea. Chris convinced me they were okay. Chris was right. She ate some food with them and I rested and had the tea, which did calm my stomach.

The next day we left the beach and headed back to the capital. When we were there, we decided to sightsee. On a city bus, I felt an arm helping me up the stairway. He was also helping himself into the zipper of my white patent leather bag. When I sat down I saw that my bag was open, the wallet and my tourist card were gone. I no longer had the ID I needed to enter and leave the country. I was panicked. "Don't worry," Chris said. "We'll go to the police." We went to the closest police station and asked for help. The chief and his assistant glared at us when they heard our story. There was some anti-American feeling. Hippies used a lot of drugs and were an annoyance in Mexico. The police resented how Mexicans were treated across the border in our country. So, we didn't think they were going to be very sympathetic and they were not. They called the U.S. embassy to check my identity and said we could leave on a train and I would not have a problem because the chief was going to call the authorities on the railroad while we were on it. They made us pay for a taxi with them in it with us enroute to the train for the border. Of course, we were hassled on the train, but eventually made it across to Texas where Chris vouched for my ID and we were issued a letter so I could take a plane home with my friend. She wanted to visit an aunt and uncle in Oklahoma before returning to New York and I agreed it was a good idea. We hadn't slept in 24 hours with all of the train travel and changing planes. Her uncle picked us up at the Tulsa airport and we went to his home where we slept until late the next day. Her uncle was a pilot and had a small plane at the airport. We took turns riding in his tiny two-seater plane. What a rush! It felt like we were birds flying in the air. We both loved it! We had a good time with her aunt and uncle for a few days. Finally, we said our goodbyes and called our parents to pick us up at Kennedy Airport.

We returned to our normal lives. Sadly, the friendship waned after a while. Chris was serious about a new boyfriend. I didn't have one. We both moved on in different directions. We did meet up and renew our friendship some years later when I was married and pregnant and Chris had been married, divorced, and was raising a little boy as a single mom.

Teaching and graduate school were beckoning. No time to breathe. I was getting more anxious to be on my own. Leave the nest. It was going to happen soon.

Chapter Thirty-One
Out on My Own

The world was changing, yet parents are prisoners of their eras. My parents were liberal politically, but conservative regarding sexual conduct. They didn't comprehend a need for independence. "What's wrong with staying home until you get married?" They were hoping that I was going to marry my second cousin, Les, my dad's cousin's son. He was probably the person my father liked the most of all my boyfriends, because he was quiet and non-confrontational, unlike the more outspoken ones I usually preferred. Marriage wasn't meant to be. I remained single and I wanted my own apartment. Why not? I could share one with another girl to offset expenses and come home on weekends. When my brother's marriage broke up before the end of the year, his apartment was available. I grabbed the opportunity. My friend, Carole, wanted to live on her own too. We signed a new lease for two years and hired movers to bring our belongings to the apartment.

My friend was a good roommate and we settled into our new routine easily. We even planned a trip to Puerto Rico and Europe together. The only glitch was a stupid mistake I made. When she was with her boyfriend in his apartment, I always told her mom that Carole would call her back later. But one night, Carole was gone for many hours and I told her mom that Carole would call back in an hour. When she didn't, her mom called our apartment and wanted to know where Carole was. I flubbed that situation miserably and both Carole and her mother were upset with me. The boyfriend became a fiancé and all was right in Carole's world again. We went to Europe, came back and her boyfriend missed her so much that she promised to move back home to be with him and plan their wedding.

Carole introduced me to a Canadian named Bernie when we were in Europe and he came with me to her wedding. Her new husband, Mark, was a stockbroker and made a lot of money. Carole did not have to continue teaching English for very long. I spoke to her a few times, but got the message that she and Mark had married friends and there was no room for a single friend in the mix. Again, I lost a good friend, but was going to find new ones.

I had to find a new roommate. I was friendly with another Spanish teacher who also was ready to leave home. She agreed to share the apartment with me and I was glad I had someone to help pay the rent.

She had a red shorthaired cat named Max and I said it was all right for him to live in the apartment with us. He was good company.

The mistake I made was being friends with a roommate. We did too much together. We worked in the same school, lived together and traveled together too. Overkill! We went to Mexico and California. The Mexico trip was fine. The trouble surfaced in California and that was my fault. I still feel guilty for what transpired.

When we were in L.A., I explained that I wanted to see my family. Aunt Sara was the fly in the ointment. She met Susan and didn't like her for superficial reasons. Susan was not very pretty or rich. I was invited to sleep in my aunt's condo and not my friend. Stupidly, I stayed with my aunt and Susan went to a hotel. What an insensitive fool I was.

We came home separately. Susan didn't speak to me. I was angry with her for some petty reason too. She decided to find another apartment in Queens. Since I couldn't pay for the rent for this apartment and the lease was ending, I started looking for cheaper apartments in Brooklyn near where I worked. Luckily, Susan worked at Lafayette High School and I was appointed to New Utrecht, another Brooklyn school. She would not have to see me again.

I talked to the Supers in each building I looked at. I found a vacant apartment in a building in Sheepshead Bay. It was across the street from a Waldbaum's Supermarket and close to the Belt Parkway. I had never been so close to where I worked before. It was a perfect location for me.

I met the neighbors on the floor. Two geeky guys were very friendly and I felt comfortable in asking them for help if I needed it. I could visit my Aunt Blanche and Uncle Irv in Brooklyn more often and they could come to my new place too. This apartment was great I thought.

Chapter Thirty-Two
Alone

I was always looking for new friends. One girlfriend, Shelly, was moving to the east coast of Florida with her parents. I never got a phone call when she moved. Nada. I would have liked to visit and see if maybe I wanted to teach school in Florida instead of New York, but it was not going to happen. I had to find friends at work. And I did. One semester, a girl my age came to the school after being excessed from South Shore High School. She was in the teachers' lounge and asked if anyone was going to Rockaway Parkway. I had to go in that direction anyway and volunteered to drive her. I continued to drop her off until her car was fixed and she no longer needed a ride. We talked and joked a lot in the car. Susan became a close friend even after she went back to her English job at South Shore. She included me in her large network of friends and I was very grateful. She was the organizer—she got us theater tickets, had parties, and invited me to join a tennis group. There were four of us in the group. We played tennis at a club in Sheepshead Bay that had indoor courts with a bubble over it for the winter. The four girls were Maryann, Pat, Susan, and me. Maryann was the only married girl. The women were terrible players, but we had fun. We enjoyed going out to eat afterwards.

Straight-laced Pat was often horrified by Susan's outrageous, loud, raucous behavior. But, she remained part of our group until she met someone, got married, and dumped Susan and the rest of us.

One afternoon, Pat had an appointment and couldn't play. Susan invited a male friend from South Shore High School to fill in. His name was Scott and he liked being with the three of us. Susan invited him to eat dinner later at her house. She was making her specialty, Moussaka. She hinted to me privately that he was a good catch for me. "The only negative is that he skis all winter and is never around on weekends." I filed that info away in my mind and was sizing him up. I had been dating a math teacher named Jerry, but we broke up. Scott had been to the same party where I met Jerry. We never said one word to each other on that occasion. He was very quiet at the party, but now he was outgoing with all the girls at

Susan's house. I thought he was nice.

Susan said he asked for my number and I told her to give it to him. He called about a week later and we liked going out together. We went out a lot, even midweek, and we ate out constantly. I wondered how he could afford it. We loved getting linzer tarts at a greasy spoon, a little dingy old-fashioned coffee shop in his neighborhood in Brighton Beach. That was our thing. We didn't get fat either. He exercised a lot and so did I and we were young—25 and 26. He did explain that he loved skiing and was away every weekend in the winter. "How hard is it to learn how to ski?" He was pleased that I showed interest in learning his passion.

My friends in the building fed my cat, Chico, when I was away every weekend. Scott was surprised that they were so accommodating. "That skinny guy really likes you. He probably hopes you'll break up with me and go out with him." "Not my type," I said.

He was patient with me learning how to ski. I cried a lot, came home and took a lot of hot baths. Skiing was a tough sport. Besides, I was terrified of heights. But, I persisted and went skiing with Scott and his friends. His friend, Steve, and girlfriend, Barbara, skied Hunter Mountain with us. She was a great athlete, a good cook, a good swimmer, and made a lot of money too. I was in awe of her. They lived in Manhattan and I loved going to the city to be with them.

Scott and I were inseparable. One evening, I made dinner for my new boyfriend. The dish was called Vatape. It was a Brazilian fish stew and very exotic I thought. Little did I know that he was pretending to eat my food, but secretly was feeding it to the cat or putting it in a napkin and throwing it out later. I got the message that either he found going out more convenient or he didn't like my cooking. So, we went out more and cooked-in seldom, if at all.

I was going to L.A. Christmastime to see my brother. He told me, "I'm skiing in California." As it turned out, there was no snow that winter in the ski area and Scott cancelled his reservations at the ski resort and came with me to L.A. He met my brother and was invited to his apartment in West Hollywood. My brother joked about his neighborhood. When we walked down the street with Dan, my cousin Bob, and I, Scott verbalized that the men made passes at Dan and Bob but not him. He and Dan traded funny remarks. Dan described the men as festive, a very funny term we thought. When we saw "Festive Cakes" in a small grocery store, we brought them to Dan as a goof.

Dan described Scott as being like our Uncle Morris—not so much in looks, but the personality, the New York attitude. They got along fine. We also met Uncle Lou, his wife Laura, and my cousins, Fran and Murray. The dinner with Lou and Laura at their house was very odd. We couldn't wait to get away. My uncle was very cold and Laura looked like a Playboy bunny, not a warm and fuzzy aunt at all. Fran and Murray were bizarre. All the guests at their Christmas party were transvestites. Murray did not seem straight either. Fran was her usual sarcastic self. I was wondering what Scott thought of my relatives. We had the chance to visit his Uncle Sandy (real name Saul) at his jewelry shop in downtown Los Angeles. Scott hadn't seen his dad's brother in years. So I wondered what kind of relationship he had with his uncle who had the same name as my Dad.

The funniest encounter was our invitation to Aunt Sara's condo. I warned Scott that she was snobbish. Sure enough, true to form, Aunt Sara served us bacon and eggs and while she asked Scott if he wanted more, she commented to me, "Too bad you brought Scott along. I would have introduced you to a doctor." He heard since he was just on the other side of her pass-through window, but he ignored her obnoxious comment and said he would like more bacon. I thought she was funny. When I was in L.A. alone the year or two before, she never introduced me to any single men. She saw a handsome young man when we stopped at a filling station for gas and started talking to him and said her niece was visiting. He was a zookeeper. Probably he had a girlfriend. He did not ask for my number. That was the closest I came to Aunt Sarah introducing me to any eligible bachelors.

We admired her paintings hung on the walls of the living room. She had done them in art classes after Uncle Harry died and she needed something to do. They were really quite nice and we complimented them. We thought it a shame that neither her son nor daughter kept them after her death many years after our visit with her.

On a free afternoon, we played tennis. Scott signed a piece of paper pledging to make our relationship more permanent some day. I kept it with the photos we took of that trip.

When we were together almost a year, I gave an ultimatum: either you are serious or I want to date other people again, I said.

Chapter Thirty-Three

1974

Giving Scott my ultimatum worked. I was tired of dating and ready for a meaningful relationship with someone I cared for. Despite my less than stellar cooking skills, Scott loved me a lot. By the latter part of the year, he had spoken to his friend, Jay, about getting a ring. His friend manufactured jewelry and had beautiful stones. Later on when we were married, I learned that Scott had cosigned a loan for him and that faux pas would come back to bite us in the ass when the business and friendship died. But, meanwhile, we were friends with him and his wife and they would become the witnesses at our tiny wedding the following year. I'm getting ahead of myself.

Scott shaved off his beard, leaving only a mustache, and rang my bell to pick me up on a Saturday night. He had a small box hidden in his hand. At first, I said, "Who are you?" when I peeked through the tiny eyehole in my door. "It's me." "Oh." This would be the first of my surprise "oh" exclamations. My family teases me about saying "oh" for everything. He came in, took off his jacket, and presented me with the ring (and the stone I preferred, a marquis shape). I was so happy. He called his parents to ask if they were going to be home. "I'm playing Mah-Jongg," his mom said. "I just got engaged." "Then, I'm home," his mother said eagerly. We went to their apartment to celebrate with some champagne his dad went out to buy.

I hadn't told my parents yet. "It can wait until tomorrow," I told Scott's parents. I thought to myself that my parents were not going to be as overjoyed. My dad didn't like any boyfriend I had except for a guy from the neighborhood I once dated and I didn't like. Also, they were not warm and affectionate to Dan's wife, Judy. But, I thought I would have a moderate wedding with all my family and friends there. It turned out not to be the case. Like wanting to go away to a state university and being told I couldn't because the college expected me to start in the summer and I had a camp job, Pop had the excuse not to send me to New Paltz. Same with a wedding—there was a deposit on a temple for December, but it wasn't going to happen. We were married in October—no wedding with friends and family and we paid for the reception at a restaurant ourselves.

My students at New Utrecht noticed the ring right away. "What's your married name going to be?" they asked.

"Same as my maiden name." That news always startled everyone who knew me.

And so it came to pass, Miss Schindler became Mrs. Schindler.

Chapter Thirty-Four
Vignettes

What my mother told me while she was baking or instructing me how to crochet or construct a clay piece registered in the recesses of my mind. Her thoughts were precious memories about her family that I pass down to you.

On one such occasion in Mom's musty basement that smelled of damp clay, she talked about her parents and their custom of going to the theater and leaving my mom alone with her sisters and brothers. She waited inside on the stairs of their house for them to come home at night. That's why today she made a small sculpture—a wall plaque in red clay that represented a small girl sitting on a flight of steps. I had the impression that my mother did not have a great deal of attention from her parents. Her older siblings had the role of parenting her. The custom at the time was to believe that "children should be seen and not heard."

Small children were not indulged in those days the way they are today.

Mom tried to tell me as much as she could about her two older brothers, Willie and Daniel, but the information was still sketchy. She gave me their hairbrushes made of tortoise shell and engraved with their initials that I keep in the spare bedroom on top of an antique oak dresser. They both died in their 20s. I thought she said one died of pneumonia, but my younger cousin, Steven William (named for William), just told me on a recent visit that they died of heart disease. That explanation makes the most sense because my mom's older sister had rheumatic fever when she was a child and was advised by her doctor not to have children because of a weak heart. I thought it was very sad that my uncles died so young. I never had the chance to know them.

I was in Mom's kitchen one afternoon and she began talking about her old neighborhood in Brooklyn. Her mother's best friend and confidante was a lady named Mrs. Messing who spent many an idle hour in my grandmother's kitchen when the ladies' husbands were at work and their children at school. The Messings owned a bakery in Brooklyn. My mother wondered if this was the same family who owned a huge baking enterprise. Was

Mrs. Messing related to a certain red-haired comedienne who was the star of a television show called Will and Grace? I never had an answer to that question nor the previous one. Our conversations predated the Internet and instant research.

We needed the intimacy and coziness of Mom's kitchen and a piece of her sherry cake to soften the impact of a painful revelation. I don't recall why the topic came up, but Mom was talking about her life when she was a teenager growing up in Brooklyn during the war years. Her mother wrote to relatives in her native Austria-Hungary (now the empire is divided into separate countries). She used to laughingly say that her mother advised, "Never trust a Hungarian," although I didn't know why. While in this vein, Mom became very serious. She said that as the situation in Europe became more intolerable for Jews, one of Grandma's relatives wrote and asked if my mother, Estelle, just a girl of maybe 16 or 17, would agree to marry a cousin so he would have passage out of Europe and into America. My mother refused to marry someone she didn't know. When Grandma no longer received mail from the family in her home country, she feared the worst had happened to all of them. Mom felt a terrible responsibility—that she caused the death of the young man. Her mother tried to convince her that it wasn't so, but my mother carried this guilt in her soul for many years. Maybe unburdening herself to me helped somewhat. I hope so.

I do know some of the family's history in bits and pieces. Grandma Yetta Karp's maiden name was Ihr, which means the month of May. When she and my grandfather, Isadore Karp, crossed the ocean and arrived on Ellis Island, it was a providential event. They almost travelled in a ship that sank two weeks before. If they hadn't changed their minds and left in that ill-fated craft, we wouldn't be here.

My Grandfather Isadore owned a furniture business in the 1920s and did very well. He and his wife had servants and a luxurious home. My mother remembers that during the depression even when they had less, they managed to survive and they gave money to men who knocked on the door and asked for odd jobs or food. My grandmother fed all of the hollow-eyed men. Sadly, my grandparents eventually lost the business and their fortune. My grandfather had Parkinson's disease and his health gradually deteriorated. I have photos of him in a wheelchair. My grandmother declined after his death and Mom said that she just tired of living. I vaguely remember being told when I was maybe four years old that my grandmother had died. Aunt Bea took care of the funeral arrangements, cleaning out the house, and selling it.

I wish I knew more about their history or my mother had written a diary. Aunt Bea had given Mom one, but there was nothing in it. Mom concentrated on art and did not write in her book at all. All I can provide is a scant portrait of what I remember.

Chapter Thirty-Five
An Intimate Circle

On one of our trips to California, an unusual reunion took place. My cousin's wife, Rima, invited one of my first cousins to visit. The men were not present in the house. My cousin, Bob, and my husband, Scott, were somewhere else. I don't recall where they went, but the women had a few hours alone.

Present were Rima, my first cousin Kim, and me. Eerily, the conversation we had with Kim was very similar to one I heard when my cousin Debbie, her half sister, spoke to Scott and me about their father, my uncle Lou, your grandfather's youngest brother. Debbie told stories about Lou's mistreatment of her and her older sister. They were afraid of him. He was very controlling and did not tolerate any non-compliance. He was livid when his wife Corinne insisted on going to college at night. She wanted to improve herself by becoming educated and earning a degree. Lou did not want his wife to be anything other than a housewife. The arguments caused a fracture in the marriage and Corinne sued for divorce. The girls continued to live with their mother in a tiny apartment in Los Angeles. They claim that he was frugal with child support and alimony. My grandparents naturally sided with their son and blamed Corinne for the divorce. She had met a man in night school and did marry him a long time after the divorce was final.

Lou had partial custody of his daughters and saw them on weekends. That's when I met them again on a visit to New York. They came to see us in the Hewlett house. I was jealous when they talked about staying in luxurious hotels in the city. My family didn't stay in fancy hotels. But, Lou took them there all for show. In reality, Lou provided very little financial support. It was a refrain I heard from their half-sister, Kim. She corroborated their complaints that he was notoriously stingy.

Kim spoke about Lou's famous temper. When she was a young teenager living with Lou and his third wife, Laura, he bellowed angrily that Kim spent an exorbitant amount of money on shampoo. She was very frightened by his behavior and tried not to anger him. I remembered that my brother, Dan, feared Lou and couldn't wait for the day when he no longer had to work for Lou in his carpet business. He took a test to become a stockbroker and left Lou's employ when he had secured his position at Dean Witter.

Rima and I talked about our family experiences, but they paled in comparison to the emotional rollercoaster the other cousins were on with Lou. I felt sorry for Kim. She had no guidance or maternal love to offset the turmoil her dad caused at home. Laura was concerned with her survival. She was asserting her independence with her domineering husband, but she feared his reaction. She wanted to work outside the home, but Lou didn't want her to. He was very jealous of his blonde, blue-eyed, attractive wife who was chronologically forty-something, but had every surgical option to create the illusion of a much younger, sexier woman. He forbade her from working. The continual arguments created tension. Kim was caught in the middle of a whirling eddy. She escaped by staying in her room.

The stage was set for tragedy. Laura plotted the murder of her abusive husband by slowing poisoning him. When he didn't die, she shot him in his sleep. Kim was away with her maternal grandparents for a weekend visit and was spared seeing her step- mother led away in handcuffs by the police. The motherless child became an orphan overnight.

Kim narrated her story in Rima's den. I listened raptly to her tale. Why was my uncle such a control freak? Why was he such a terrible father? My own father was controlling, but not violent. Nor was their sister, Sarah, Rima's mother-in-law. What traits did he inherit from my paternal grandparents? My grandfather was so gentle. I laid the blame on my grandmother, not knowing if there was any validity to my hunch.

One story I heard about my Grandmother Rose was decidedly unflattering. She had four children and didn't want to be pregnant again. But what was an immigrant woman to do without birth control or abortion as an option? The legend was that Grandma stood on a dining room chair and jumped off to self-abort the baby. We laughed, but it was no laughing matter. Maybe Lou was psychologically damaged by not being wanted by his own mother. Who knows? Vere Vaist? (Yiddish for who knows?)

I saw Kim only one more time and did not have such an in-depth conversation with her. Rima's daughter, Larisa, had a bat mitzvah and Kim was invited, but was only able to come to the temple service and not the party at night. I think she was unable to get a babysitter for her infant son. She was happy and seemed to be enjoying her life with her baby and had a good job as a mortgage broker. We took pictures together.

At that time, we both had auburn hair with a little help from our hair- dressers.

Kim's fate was not unforeseen. Her mother and father died violent deaths and so did she at the hands of an abusive boyfriend—no trial. He killed her and himself. Kim's son followed in her footsteps, becoming an orphan at age four.

It's a strange legacy on the Schindler side. All I can say is you have to appreciate life, value your one brother, and maintain contact with the c ousins you know and love. Live life to the fullest and don't sweat the small stuff.

Photo Gallery

Me, Aunt Blanche at his Bar Mitzvah, 1959

Pop, roadtrip in 1950's

Pop and Mom, 1941

Our home, Laurelton, N.Y., 1950's

Mom, me and Pop at Bryce Canyon, 1958

(front row) Grandpa, Lou, Bob, friend
(standing) Aunt Sara, Aunt Shirley

Grandma, me, Grandpa, in front of our building, 1958

Cousin's Debbie and Andrea, 1950's

Danny and Aunt Bea, Summer 1958

Me in Washington, D.C., 1970's

Me in Switzerland, 1970's

Helendez Hotel, Taxco, Mexico, August 1969

www.ingramcontent.com/pod-product-compliance
Lightning Source LLC
Chambersburg PA
CBHW051447250726
48655CB00001B/283